Praise for
The Divine Defense

"In *The Divine Defense,* Robert Jeffress equips the believer with a clear and practical battle strategy for the ideals we hold sacred. I highly recommend this latest from one of Christianity's leading pastor-teachers."

—DR. ED YOUNG, pastor, Second Baptist Church in Houston, Texas, and author of *Romancing the Home* and *The Ten Commandments of Marriage*

"If you can only read one book in 2006, this is it, and for all your remaining years of spiritual service, you will be glad you did."

—CHAPLAIN (COL) GIL A. STRICKLIN, USA, RETIRED, founder and president, Marketplace Chaplains USA and International

"Suit up and step up! Robert Jeffress has written a book about truths that should be both in our heads and hearts to prepare us for spiritual battle. Intensively biblical. Useful in the day by day. This is one book I'm sure to reread on numerous occasions."

—DR. MARK L. BAILEY, president, Dallas Theological Seminary

"A balanced look at spiritual warfare, giving us a concrete plan for success in the spirit realm. Dr. Jeffress pulls back the curtain and helps us see that high stakes battle raging in the 'fifth dimension,' and *The Divine Defense* shows how we can keep Satan on the run as we wage the spirit wars!"

—RANDY SINGER, author of *The Cross Examination of Jesus Christ* and its companion novel, *The Cross Examination of Oliver Finney*

"Struggling with life's challenges? *The Divine Defense* is the answer! Robert Jeffress identifies the enemy, exposes his strategies, reinforces our defenses, and motivates us to victory. Don't miss this book with what you need to know to win—and win big!"

—DR. ED HINDSON, assistant chancellor, Liberty University

"Robert Jeffress has provided a great resource for Christians living in a fast-paced world. You will be reminded as to the *why* of the distress in and around you as well as the *how* to mute the agitation. The truth is our enemy doesn't have a prayer—and this book will help you practice that truth."

—NEIL ATKINSON, AUTHOR OF *THE SHREWD CHRISTIAN*

"A biblical and balanced approach to dealing with Satan and defeating spiritual enemies. This book is a call to arms that we may experience true victory in Jesus."

—DR. JACK GRAHAM, pastor, Prestonwood Baptist Church,
and author with Chuck Norris of *A Man of God*

"Dr. Robert Jeffress has done it again. He provides *The Divine Defense* available to every believer—and he does so in a captivating and strategic manner with positive application. As in the old and oft repeated hymn, *The Divine Defense* will lead you to 'Put on the gospel armor; each piece put on with prayer.'"

—DR. O.S. HAWKINS, president, GuideStone Financial Resources

"In an age that either denies the existence of Satan and his cohorts or is overly fascinated with and engaged in the occult, Robert Jeffress provides the church with a sober, sensible, practical, Bible-based manual full of practical steps to find victory over demonic protagonists."

—DR. EUGENE H. MERRILL, distinguished professor of Old Testament
Studies, Dallas Theological Seminary

"In all too many cases, books dealing with spiritual warfare tend to lean toward the superficial side of the bizarre. *The Divine Defense*, however, goes right to the heart of the biblical text and deals with the spiritual warfare that is at the very center of the Christian life, describing the reality of the battle but pointing to the victory achieved through Jesus Christ. This is an important book for our times and the church."

—DR. AL MOHLER, president, Southern Baptist Theological Seminary

THE DIVINE DEFENSE

ALSO BY ROBERT JEFFRESS

Grace Gone Wild!
Coming Home
Hell? Yes! And Other Outrageous Truths You Can Still Believe
The Solomon Secrets
Hearing the Master's Voice
When Forgiveness Doesn't Make Sense
I Want More!

THE DIVINE DEFENSE

SIX SIMPLE STRATEGIES FOR WINNING YOUR GREATEST BATTLES

ROBERT JEFFRESS

THE DIVINE DEFENSE

All Scripture quotations, unless otherwise indicated, are taken from the New American Standard Bible® (NASB). © Copyright The Lockman Foundation 1960, 1962, 1963, 1968, 1971, 1972, 1973, 1975, 1977, 1995. Used by permission. (www.Lockman.org). Scripture quotations marked (KJV) are taken from the King James Version. Scripture quotations marked (TLB) are taken from The Living Bible, copyright © 1971. Used by permission of Tyndale House Publishers Inc., Wheaton, Illinois 60189. Scripture quotations marked (NIV) are taken from the Holy Bible, New International Version®. NIV®. Copyright © 1973, 1978, 1984 by International Bible Society. Used by permission of Zondervan Publishing House. All rights reserved. Scripture quotations marked (NLT) are taken from the Holy Bible, New Living Translation, copyright © 1996. Used by permission of Tyndale House Publishers Inc., Wheaton, Illinois 60189. All rights reserved. Scripture quotations marked (Phillips) are taken from The New Testament in Modern English, Revised Edition © 1972 by J. B. Phillips. Copyright renewed © 1986, 1988 by Vera M. Phillips.

Italics in Scripture quotations indicate the author's added emphasis.

Details in some anecdotes and stories have been changed to protect the identities of the persons involved.

Trade Paperback ISBN 978-1-4000-7090-9
eBook ISBN 978-0-307-49960-8

Copyright © 2006 by Robert Jeffress

Published in association with Yates & Yates, LLP, Attorneys and Counselors, Orange, California.

Published in the United States by WaterBrook, an imprint of the Crown Publishing Group, a division of Penguin Random House LLC, New York

WATERBROOK® and its deer colophon are registered trademarks of Penguin Random House LLC.

Library of Congress Cataloging-in-Publication Data
Jeffress, Robert, 1955–
    The divine defense : six simple strategies for winning your greatest battles / Robert Jeffress. — 1st ed.
        p. cm.
    ISBN-13: 978-1-4000-7090-9
    1. Spiritual warfare. I. Title.
    BV4509.5.J435 2006
    235'.4—dc22

                                                          2006015239

Printed in the United States of America

SPECIAL SALES
Most WaterBrook books are available in special quantity discounts when purchased in bulk by corporations, organizations and special interest groups. Custom imprinting or excerpting can also be done to fit special needs. For information, please e-mail specialmarketscms@penguinrandomhouse.com or call 1-800-603-7051.

To Dr. Venkat Thota and his godly wife, Lakshmi Thota

You and your family are living testimonies of God's grace and a continuing encouragement to your pastor. Thank you for your vision for spreading the timeless truths of God's Word throughout the world.

CONTENTS

PART ONE: UNDERSTANDING YOUR ENEMY

1. The Other World 3
   It's what you can't see that can hurt you

2. The Purpose-Driven Strife 15
   How a war that began long ago affects you today

3. Blueprint for Your Destruction 31
   Satan's threefold plan for ruining your life

4. Demons in the World Today 53
   Satan's sidekicks are no laughing matter

5. What Demons Want to Do to You 63
   Satan hates you and has a terrible plan for your life

6. Winning the Mind Games 75
   You are what you think

7. Satan's Favorite Mind Games 87
   Four lies that will pull you away from God

PART TWO: STRATEGIES FOR SUCCESS
IN THE DIVINE DEFENSE

8. When Satan Comes Knocking 99
   Strategy 1: Recognize and replace destructive thoughts

9. Putting Out the Not Welcome Mat 107
   Strategy 2: Do what you know you should do

10. Putting on Your Soul Soles 127
    Strategy 3: Make God's business your business

11. Storming the Gates of Hell 147
Strategy 4: Move forward in spite of your doubts
Strategy 5: Remember your power to win
Strategy 6: Strengthen your resolve to resist

PART THREE: LIVING THE DIVINE DEFENSE

12. Exercise Power or Exorcise Demons? 165
Beware of the Weird
13. Using the Divine Defense 175
Six effective ways to keep Satan on the run

Questions. 189
For personal study or small-group discussion

Notes 199

For we are not fighting against people made of flesh and blood,
but against the evil rulers and authorities of the unseen world,
against those mighty powers of darkness who rule this world,
and against the wicked spirits in the heavenly realms.

EPHESIANS 6:12 (NLT)

PART ONE

UNDERSTANDING YOUR ENEMY

The Other World

It's what you can't see that can hurt you

> We are not human beings having a spiritual experience,
> but we are spiritual beings having a human experience.
> —Pierre Teilhard de Chardin

There is a fifth dimension beyond that which is known to man. It is a dimension as vast as space and as timeless as infinity. It is the middle ground between light and shadow, between science and superstition. It lies between the pit of man's fears and the summit of his knowledge. This is the dimension of imagination. It is an area which we call *the twilight zone.*"

Every Friday night during the early 1960s I would listen to Rod Serling's voice as he introduced his TV program, *The Twilight Zone.* The anthology series dealt with that middle ground where the visible and invisible forces in the universe intersect each other.

Each week, ordinary people would discover a fifth dimension of reality invading their everyday experiences. Those of us who grew up watching *The Twilight Zone* will always remember certain episodes: the airline passenger who looks out his window one stormy night and sees a demonic creature on the aircraft wing destroying the engines; the customer who realizes the mannequins in a department store were once human beings; or the father who discovers that his life is a motion picture and he's only an actor playing his part.

Beyond the natural entertainment value of the show, the appeal of *The*

Twilight Zone (and the other sci-fi programs that it spawned) was that it tapped into an instinct we all have that there is something more to life than what we can see or measure. How else do we explain:

- the coincidences we experience that cannot be attributed to mere chance?
- the intuitive feelings we experience that turn out to be correct?
- the random impulses we feel to do something completely out of character?
- the sensations we have when we're alone that we are *not* alone?

Rod Serling was right. There is another world that is beyond human comprehension. This other world is as vast as space and as timeless as infinity. This other world is the spirit world. It is the realm where God, Satan, angels, and demons reside. And whether you realize it or not, it is the reality that is responsible for most of the struggles you experience every day of your life.

Although this other world is invisible and immeasurable, it is in truth more real and more permanent than the visible world in which we exist. The Bible assures us that one day everything we can see, feel, and touch will be consumed by fire. All that will remain will be our spirits, which will be given new bodies to inhabit and a new heaven and earth in which to reside for all eternity. As philosopher Pierre Teilhard de Chardin wrote, "We are not human beings having a spiritual experience, but we are spiritual beings having a human experience."[1]

I realize that not everyone accepts that proposition. Admittedly, it's difficult to believe in something that isn't empirically verifiable. Randy Alcorn imagines a discussion between twins in their mother's womb the day before they're born.

"You know," one says, "there's a whole world out there—grassy meadows and snowy mountains, splashing streams and waterfalls, horses and dogs and cats and whales and giraffes. There are skyscrapers and cities and people like us, only much bigger, playing games like football and baseball and volleyball and going to the beach."

"Are you crazy?" the other twin responds. "That's just wishful thinking. Everybody knows that there's no such thing as life after birth."[2]

Such a limited perspective is the by-product of naturalism that is often—and erroneously—equated with "science." A naturalist is one who believes that nature is all that there is. He is convinced that only what is visible and measurable is real. His worldview leaves no room for the supernatural, which by definition refers to those things that are above, beyond, or in addition to the natural world that can be seen and measured.

Unfortunately for the naturalist, science itself has demonstrated the inherent weakness in his perspective. Only recently in man's long history have we discovered the reality of germs, atoms, and electricity, all of which have been present in the universe since creation. Just because man was not able to see or measure those realities for thousands of years, were they any less real? To limit reality to the visible and measurable leads to a kind of tunnel vision unnecessarily limiting our ability to see the world, and our own lives, as they really are.

Nikos Kazantzakis described two artists engaged in a contest to see who could most accurately paint a picture portraying the visible world.

"Now I shall prove to you that I am the best," said the first artist, pointing to a curtain he had painted.

"Well, draw back the curtain, and let us see the picture," the second artist requested.

"The curtain is the picture," replied the first painter with a laugh.[3]

Behind the curtain of our visible existence is a world more real and more enduring than the one we can see. But what is that world like? And what is our place in that world?

WAR OF THE WORLDS

Although this parallel world is invisible to the naked eye, as it also is to the most powerful microscope or telescope, we do possess an instrument that allows us to peek behind the curtain. Through the lens of the Bible, we discover there is an unseen war raging between the forces of good and evil. Gregory Boyd describes that conflict this way:

> The truth to which all these [elements] point…is the truth that God's good creation has in fact been seized by hostile, evil cosmic forces that are seeking to destroy God's beneficent plan for the cosmos.… The general assumption of both the Old and New Testaments is that the earth is virtually engulfed by cosmic forces of destruction, and that evil and suffering are ultimately due to this diabolical siege.… God waged war against these forces, however, and through the person of Jesus Christ has now secured the overthrow of this cosmic army. The church as the body of Christ has been called to be a decisive means by which this final overthrow is to be carried out.[4]

In the next chapter we will discover the origin of this cosmic seizure of "God's good creation" as well as its ultimate outcome. But why do those of us who may be worrying about surviving the next round of layoffs at work, making our mortgage payment next month, or navigating our children through adolescence need to concern ourselves with some unseen spiritual war?

WHEN THE OTHER WORLD INVADES YOURS

Do you remember September 11, 2001, when the first jet slammed into the north tower of the World Trade Center in New York City? I was drinking my final cup of coffee before work. The morning news program I was watching was interrupted to broadcast live pictures of a gaping hole in one of the world's tallest buildings. The commentators speculated endlessly about the cause of the so-called accident. In fact, when President George W. Bush was told about the crash, he reportedly said, "That's some bad pilot!"

Many of us felt the same way. If indeed the crash had been caused by pilot error, perhaps the remedy for future accidents would have been to order remedial training for pilots, better navigation systems installed in planes, or more skilled air-traffic controllers at airports. But we soon discovered it was no accident. When another plane crashed into the second tower, we immediately knew that America was under attack from a hostile force. For the first time in more than one hundred years, an enemy attack on our own continent forced us to quickly formulate a strategy for defeating the new adversary.

Knowing the source of a problem is crucial for developing a strategy to combat that problem. A navigational accident demands one response. A hostile strike requires a completely different strategy.

Every day our world is invaded by what are commonly thought to be random events, and we respond accordingly.

Couples divorce, so we develop marriage enrichment seminars.

Drug use among children increases, so we educate them about the dangers of narcotics and encourage them to "just say no."

Use of pornography rises dramatically among Christians, so we organize accountability groups.

Churches fight and threaten to split, so we hire arbitrators to help with conflict resolution.

Christians complain of depression and thoughts of suicide, so we medicate them with the latest drugs.

Please understand, I'm all for marriage seminars, drug education, accountability groups, conflict resolution, and psychiatric medication when necessary. But what if the source of our problems is something more than random events? What if the explanation for the problems that assault us regularly is something other than "stuff happens"? What if we are, indeed, under enemy attack? Would we change our strategy, or at least adapt it, to confront such a reality?

MEET YOUR *REAL* ENEMY

The Bible allows us to lift the curtain on our visible existence so we can see the world as it really is. Through the lens of Scripture, we discover that not only is there an unseen world but it is a world at war. In what is perhaps the seminal passage in the New Testament about this spiritual conflict, the apostle Paul writes:

> For our struggle is not against flesh and blood, but against the rulers, against the powers, against the world forces of this darkness, against the spiritual forces of wickedness in the heavenly places. (Ephesians 6:12)

Notice Paul's use of the personal pronoun *our*. This war is not just a spat between two cosmic forces having little to do with us. We cannot shrug our shoulders when we read about it and spout a favorite Texan expression, "I don't have a dog in that fight." We *do* have a stake in this battle. Why? Whether you realize it or not, you're living in the cross fire of this spiritual war. A friend of mine said, "We Christians are not living on this earth as carefree tourists. We are soldiers on raw, pagan soil. Everywhere around us the battle rages."[5]

Those who dismiss such words as being over the top, sensational, or simply secondary to more-important spiritual realities do so to their own detriment. The late pastor David Martyn Lloyd-Jones bluntly reminds us:

> Not to realize that you are in a conflict means one thing only, and it is that you are so hopelessly defeated and so "knocked out" as it were, that you do not even know it—you are completely defeated by the devil. Anyone who is not aware of a fight and a conflict in a spiritual sense is in a drugged and hazardous condition.[6]

Admittedly, most Christians are not aware of this intense battle in which we're engaged. Although we regularly witness the fallout of the Enemy's assaults all around us—broken marriages, wayward children, divided churches, inexplicable acts of violence—we fail to connect the dots and understand the source of many of our conflicts.

There is a war raging around us and within us. As Stu Weber states, "Every Christian is a walking battlefield."[7] Pastor Steve Lawson describes the war within our hearts as a life-and-death struggle:

Deep within the hidden recesses of the human heart, a bloodless battle is being fought—a life-and-death struggle for the soul. This intense spiritual warfare is raging between God and Satan upon the invisible battlefields of our hearts. As long as we are upon this earth, every square inch of space and every split second of time in our lives is an arena of war. This battle is relentless and ruthless. It stalks us like prey. It tracks us down like a wild animal. It finds us no matter where we go. There is no escaping this war. We can't run from it. We can't hide from it. There is no neutral ground in this conflict. No truce can be called. No cease-fire negotiated. No peace treaty signed. No white flag waved. No demilitarized zone entered.[8]

In case you think all this talk of spiritual warfare is symptomatic of some kind of spiritual paranoia, consider the numerous passages in the Bible that use the imagery of war to describe our existence on earth. The first allusion to Christ in the Bible is that of an injured warrior (see Genesis 3:15). The final picture of Christ in the Bible is that of a conquering soldier who returns to Earth to reclaim His kingdom (see Revelation 19). Between the first and second comings of Christ, His followers are described as foot soldiers who are fighting for the establishment of His kingdom on the foreign soil of planet Earth.

> For the *weapons* of our *warfare* are not of the flesh, but divinely powerful for the *destruction* of *fortresses*. We are *destroying* speculations and every lofty thing raised up against the knowledge of God, and we are *taking every thought captive* to the obedience of Christ. (2 Corinthians 10:4–5)

> Put on the *full armor* of God, so that you will be able to stand firm against the schemes of the devil. For our *struggle* is not against flesh and blood, but against the *rulers*, against the *powers*, against the world *forces* of this darkness, against the spiritual *forces* of wickedness in the heavenly places. (Ephesians 6:11–12)

But I thought it necessary to send to you Epaphroditus, my brother
and fellow worker and *fellow soldier.* (Philippians 2:25)

This command I entrust to you, Timothy,...that...you *fight* the *good
fight.* (1 Timothy 1:18)

Suffer hardship with me, as a good *soldier* of Christ Jesus. No *soldier*
in active service entangles himself in the affairs of everyday life, so
that he may please the one who enlisted him as a *soldier.* (2 Timothy
2:3–4)

At some point, we need to decide whether or not we believe—really
believe—that the biblical worldview is correct. If we are convinced the Bible
is God's Word, then we must conclude that we are living in the cross fire of a
great cosmic battle.

Furthermore, we cannot claim neutrality in this war. To say "I'm a lover,
not a fighter" is no excuse for passivity. There is no safe place on the sidelines
for us to sit out the battle until the all-clear signal is sounded. Jesus made it
clear there is no allowance for conscientious objectors in this war. "He who is
not with Me is against Me," He said (Luke 11:23).

You're in the Army Now

I remember singing a rousing little chorus when I was a youngster in Sunday
school:

I may never march in the infantry,
ride in the cavalry,
shoot the artillery.
I may never zoom o'er the enemy,
but I'm in the Lord's army. Yes sir! [9]

Behind that simple song is a profound truth. You and I have been drafted to serve in a life-and-death battle for the future of the universe. Understanding that our Commander in Chief has enlisted us to serve in this cosmic war helps us remember our purpose in life and keeps us from needless distractions that would hinder our service to God. It also will encourage us to fight with every ounce of energy we have, so when our tour of duty is complete, we, like the apostle Paul, can say:

> I have fought the good fight, I have finished the course, I have kept the
> faith; in the future there is laid up for me the crown of righteousness,
> which the Lord, the righteous Judge, will award to me on that day;
> and not only to me, but also to all who have loved His appearing.
> (2 Timothy 4:7–8)

Beyond some future reward for our service to God, there is a more immediate reason to awaken from our "drugged and hazardous condition" and comprehend the spiritual war in which we are engaged. As a Christian, you are in the cross hairs of the Enemy's artillery. Whether you believe you are living in the middle of a cosmic war between God and Satan is immaterial to the devil. In fact, he prefers that you stay oblivious to the real battle raging in the universe and to your place in that battle. Like any combatant, Satan always operates more efficiently in the darkness than in the light. He has placed a giant *X* on your back and has marked you for destruction. The less aware you are of his goal, the more certain he is of success. Regardless of your level of awareness, you do have an enemy intent on destroying you.

The apostle Peter does not warn you to be on the alert and of sober spirit because *God's* adversary, the devil, prowls about. Instead, Peter describes Satan as "*your* adversary, the devil" (1 Peter 5:8). Frankly, this is one of the consequences of becoming a Christian that is rarely discussed. Before you became a believer, you were part of Satan's kingdom. You were his indentured servant and existed to serve his purpose. But when you trusted in Christ as your Savior, you were delivered "from the domain of darkness, and transferred…to the kingdom of His beloved Son" (Colossians 1:13). You have been freed from Satan's tyrannical reign and maniacal plan for your life. That's the good news.

The not-so-good news is that as part of God's kingdom His enemies have become your enemies. God's chief antagonist is now your chief adversary. John Eldredge vividly describes the conflict:

> God now has an enemy…and so do we. Man is not born into a sitcom or a soap opera; he is born into a world at war. This is not *Home Improvement*; it's *Saving Private Ryan*. There will be many, many battles to fight on many different battlefields.[10]

Before you get discouraged and think, *I'm not sure I'm up to the fight*, you should know that Satan is already a conquered opponent. In the next chapter we will discover how and when his defeat occurred. Nevertheless, in spite of the certainty of Satan's ultimate demise, he is still a powerful adversary capable of inflicting great harm. Satan possesses the power to:

- disrupt your marriage
- discourage you from trusting in God's faithfulness
- destroy your physical and mental health
- deceive your children into following him rather than God
- divide your church
- damage your influence for Christ's kingdom
- deny you of eternal rewards in heaven

Time for the Crucifix and the Garlic Necklace?

Perhaps you're one of those people who is understandably skeptical about the whole subject of spiritual warfare. You believe in the existence of Satan. You're aware of the reality of demons. You sense there is a battle going on between the forces of good and evil. You'd like to protect yourself and your loved ones from Satan's assaults.

But you're not sure what, if anything, you can do about it. You sure don't want to engage in anything weird, like trying to exorcise demons from your friends and family members. Spinning heads, levitating bodies, and creepy voices are beyond your comfort zone. You don't want to be one of those people who attributes every problem in life from cancer or hangnails to satanic attacks. Carrying a giant cross or wearing a string of garlic to ward off the evil spirits isn't for you.

If you have reservations about the subject of spiritual warfare, this book is for you. Christians tend to go to one of two extremes when it comes to the subject of spiritual warfare. Those who are unaware and, therefore, unprepared to fight the real battle that Satan is waging against them are destined to become spiritual road kill. Others become so fixated on Satan and his minions that they become demon *obsessed.*

Pastor Kent Hughes recounts a spiritual revival that touched a number of professional families in a large city years ago. When a group of doctors, lawyers, and business executives gained a new interest in Bible study, their marriages were restored and churches were energized by their spiritual fervor. But some of the leadership of the renewal movement, fascinated by the subject of spiritual warfare, started giving more attention to the work of Satan against them than the work of Christ for them.

One night their group became convinced that demons had inhabited the chandelier in the dining room where they were meeting. They concluded their Bible study by disassembling the light fixture so they could take the parts of the chandelier and bury them in different parts of the city. Not long afterward some of the children of these leaders were seen running down the street shouting, "The devil is going to get us, the devil is going to get us."[11]

Satan is just as pleased by those who obsess about him as by those who ignore him. In his classic work *The Screwtape Letters,* C. S. Lewis makes a profound observation:

> There are two equal and opposite errors into which our race can fall
> about the devils. One is to disbelieve in their existence. The other is to

believe, and to feel an excessive and unhealthy interest, in them. They [Satan and his demons] are equally pleased by both errors.[12]

The Divine Defense is written for those of you who may be unaware, or just wary, of the subject of spiritual warfare. In our journey together we will seek to be both intensely biblical and extremely practical as we discover what we can do to protect our faith, our families, and our future from the powerful attacks of our enemy. But even though Satan and his forces are real and powerful, we need not fear them, nor do we need to become obsessed with them.

Author Neil Anderson compares the world of Satan and his demons to the world of germs. We know that germs, though invisible, are all around us, he says. They inhabit our food, our water, our air, and other people with whom we come in contact. Some people are absolutely phobic about germs and spend their lives trying to insulate themselves from any contact with them. But the right diet, appropriate rest and exercise, and simple principles of hygiene will protect us from most infections. We don't have to obsess about germs to be free from them. Yet without an awareness of these microbes and the ways to protect ourselves from them, we would be more prone to illness and death.[13]

Yes, we need to exercise balance in our understanding of this complex subject of spiritual warfare. But please don't equate the word *balance* with the word *passive*.

The ancient warrior Sun Tzu observed that the art of war is of vital importance. "[War] is a matter of life and death," he said, "a road either to safety or to ruin. Hence, under no circumstances can it be ignored."[14]

You are in the middle of an invisible, though very real, war.

The stakes are high.

Your enemy is skilled, armed, and determined.

The possibility of losing everything important to you is real.

You must be aware of and prepared for the fight.

In the pages that follow, we will discover how you can win the greatest battle of your life.

THE PURPOSE-DRIVEN STRIFE

How a war that began long ago affects you today

> Enemy-occupied territory—that is
> what this world is.
> —C. S. Lewis

T here are no small parts, just small actors." Those words, spoken by legendary movie director Alfred Hitchcock, consoled me before my one big
scene in the old TV series *Dallas*. A few months earlier I'd read in the newspaper that the casting director for the popular program was looking for extras
for an episode to be shot on location in the show's namesake city. Since I lived
nearby and enjoyed watching the program every Friday night, I took a chance
and mailed in my photograph.

A few weeks later I received a call informing me I had been selected and
instructing me to be at a Dallas hotel early the next morning for the shoot.
When I arrived, I was quickly introduced to the difference between major players and extras. Major players had their own trailers for dressing rooms, while
extras were told to change in the bathrooms in the hotel lobby. But I wasn't
going to allow such a slight to diminish my excitement over my role in one of
television's highest-rated dramas.

The assistant director informed me and another extra that we were to play
businessmen having lunch in a local restaurant. The main action in the scene

was a conversation at the bar between two of the principal characters (Bobby Ewing and Cliff Barnes). Our job was to sit at a table directly behind the bar and look like we were carrying on a conversation. This leads to another distinction between major players and extras. Major players actually get to speak out loud. Extras are only allowed to move their lips to simulate speaking so that their words do not distract from the actors' dialogue (all that muffled background conversation you hear is dubbed in later).

We all assumed our positions. The director yelled, "Action!" and we began playing our parts. After about twenty seconds, the director said "Cut. Moving on." The assistant director said to my lunch companion and me, "Thank you very much. Your check will be mailed in a few days."

It was over.

For an instant, I'd been part of the legendary TV conflict between the Ewing and the Barnes families, a conflict that had begun many years earlier and that would continue for years afterward. One brief scene, a little bit of action, the promise of a check, and my part was complete—not unlike life itself.

Whether you realize it or not, you have a part to play in a major drama that began years before you were born and will continue for years after you die. Compared to the two major characters in this epic, your role may be relatively minor. Compared to eternity, your time on earth's stage is relatively brief. At your appointed time, you play the part assigned to you for however many years, and then you exit. Your future rewards depend on how well you performed your job.

But unlike my brief acting stint, the drama in which you've been cast is real; it's a story about a war that began in heaven years ago between the two most powerful (though far from equal) beings in the universe. The conflict involved a collision between two wills: the will of God and the will of His former chief of staff, Satan (originally named Lucifer).

This drama continues to play out every day on the front pages of every newspaper, as well as within the inner recesses of every human heart. You'll never comprehend the reason for the battles you face every hour of every day until you understand the origin of this war and the Enemy's goal in the war.

Satan Is Real and Really Dangerous

Some people refuse to believe in the existence of a literal devil. Ken Woodward, writing in *Newsweek* magazine, refers to Satan as "merely a trivial personification hardly adequate to symbolize the mystery of evil."[1] Others attempt to diminish Satan's power by reducing him to a comic-book character with a red suit, horns, and a tail who runs around poking people in the backside with a pitchfork. Some historians argue that this absurd caricature originated in the Middle Ages as an attempt to attack Satan by assaulting his oversized ego. How better to insult an egomaniac than to reduce him to such a ridiculous-looking icon of evil?

If that was the goal, I'm afraid the plan backfired badly.

Today many people laugh at Satan rather than fear him. Think of comedian Dana Carvey's Church Lady from the *Saturday Night Live* TV program and her signature line: "Could it be *Satan*?"

I believe the devil is delighted when people underestimate his power either by denying his existence or by diminishing his potential threat. If we're going to win this very real battle that threatens everything and everyone important to us, we must understand the ferocity of our adversary. J. Dwight Pentecost reminds us how important this is:

> No military commander could expect to be victorious in battle unless he understood his enemy. Should he prepare for an attack by land and ignore the possibility that the enemy might approach by air or by sea, he would open the way to defeat. Or should he prepare for a land and sea attack and ignore the possibility of an attack through the air, he would certainly jeopardize the campaign. No individual can be victorious against the adversary of our souls unless he understands that

adversary; unless he understands his philosophy, his methods of operation, and his methods of temptation.[2]

In this chapter we're going to unmask our most dangerous enemy by discovering his origin, examining his initial rebellion against God, and revealing his ultimate objective in your life.

A LONG TIME AGO AND FAR, FAR AWAY

Satan is the opposite of God. True or false? Sadly, many Christians would answer, "True." They view Satan as God's evil twin. They picture both beings as all powerful and all knowing. Many Christians view God and Satan's conflict as a supernatural game of tug of war in which each participant is straining to gain the advantage over the other while the rest of us sit on the sidelines hoping that "the best man wins." Nothing could be further from the truth.

"Even from everlasting to everlasting, You are God," Moses declared in a prayer recorded in Psalm 90:2. Unlike God, who is eternal and has no beginning or end, Satan has both a beginning and an end. (Several times in this chapter I refer to Satan's end and destruction. This isn't to suggest that Satan will ever cease to exist. Like human beings who die apart from Christ, Satan will suffer eternal torment in the lake of fire and brimstone as clearly stated in Revelation 20:10. By *end* and *destruction* I mean the end of his rule as the god of this world.)

Satan's origin is described in the Old Testament prophecy of Ezekiel. In the first ten verses of Ezekiel 28, the prophet is instructed to deliver a message against the king of Tyre, whose pride had led him to believe he was a god himself. But beginning in verse 12, it's clear that God is speaking to someone other than the human king:

You had the seal of perfection,
Full of wisdom and perfect in beauty.
You were in Eden, the garden of God;
Every precious stone was your covering:

The ruby, the topaz, and the diamond....

You were the anointed cherub who covers,

And I placed you there.

You were on the holy mountain of God....

You were blameless in your ways

From the day you were created

Until unrighteousness was found in you....

Your heart was lifted up because of your beauty;

You corrupted your wisdom by reason of your splendor.

I cast you to the ground;

I put you before kings,

That they may see you. (Ezekiel 28:12–15, 17)

The human leader of Tyre did not possess "the seal of perfection." No one, except perhaps his mother, would have thought of him as an "anointed cherub." And he ruled in Tyre, not on "the holy mountain of God."

God was clearly speaking to the one who had inspired the king of Tyre to rebel against God: the being we commonly call Satan (from the Hebrew word for "adversary") or the devil (from the Greek word for "slanderer").

Originally, Satan had a much more appealing name. He was called Lucifer, the Latin translation of his name found in Isaiah 14:12, meaning "star of the morning." We can piece together Lucifer's story from God's pronouncement against him in Ezekiel 28. For consistency, we will refer to him as Satan from this point on—and look at four facts about him:

- **Satan is a created being.** God uses the phrase "the day you were created" to remind Satan that, unlike God, he is a creature, not the Creator. Besides putting Satan in his place, this phrase underscores to all of us Satan's limitations. He is not omniscient (all knowing), omnipotent (all powerful), or omnipresent (able to be everywhere at once). Furthermore, just as a disgruntled deacon once reminded me, "God can say to Satan, 'I was here before you came, and I will be here after you are gone.'" That's the downside of being a creature.

- **Satan held an impressive office in God's kingdom.** Satan is referred to as "the anointed cherub" and the "cherub who covers." The term *cherub* doesn't mean that he possessed plump, pink cheeks. Instead, *cherub* refers to a rank of angels who were charged with guarding the holiness of God. Since Satan was the anointed cherub, he was evidently in charge of all the other angels who held this important office. As the one who protected the holiness and majesty of God, he was the chief gatekeeper in heaven, meaning he had unparalleled access to God.

- **Satan possessed incomparable wisdom and beauty.** God describes Satan as "full of wisdom and perfect in beauty." Although Satan's rebellion forced him to surrender his position in heaven, he did not relinquish these impressive attributes. He is still a crafty and appealing creature, making him all the more dangerous as we will discover in succeeding chapters.

- **Satan's pride led to his downfall.** Forgetting that he was a creature, Satan allowed inward pride to metastasize into outright rebellion against God. This led to an open war in heaven that continues to this day.

BATTLE OF THE WILLS

Although Ezekiel hints at the reason for Satan's rebellion against God, Isaiah gives us a blow-by-blow description of the event that led to his ouster from heaven. Like Ezekiel's prophecy against the king of Tyre, Isaiah's words represent not only God's condemnation of a human leader (in this case the king of Babylon) but the one who had inspired the king's defiant attitude toward God. The Babylonian monarch's unbridled ambition was both similar to and rooted in Satan's desire to exalt himself above God:

> How you have fallen from heaven,
> O star of the morning, son of the dawn!
> You have been cut down to the earth,

You who have weakened the nations!
But you said in your heart,
"I will ascend to heaven;
I will raise my throne above the stars of God,
And I will sit on the mount of assembly
In the recesses of the north.
I will ascend above the heights of the clouds;
I will make myself like the Most High." (Isaiah 14:12–14)

Perhaps it had been building over a period of time. Maybe it happened after Lucifer attended a motivational seminar or finished reading a new book on leadership.

Whatever the stimulus, Satan closed his eyes and said to himself: *I don't have to stay the person I am. All I have to do is determine what I want to be and then dedicate myself to doing whatever it takes to become that person.* Then Satan looked around and began dreaming about future possibilities.

Instead of being just one of many angels, I want to rule over all the angels.

Instead of having to bow down before that spoiled son of God, I want to sit on his throne and have him worship me for a change.

When I think about it, what I really want is to be like God.

Prior to Satan's conversation with himself, there had been only one will in heaven, and that was God's will. But that one will became two wills when Satan decided to pursue an agenda separate from God's purpose for him. The Bible does not explain how a perfect creature like Satan could have an imperfect thought that would lead to a wide-scale rebellion. Theologians refer to it as "the mystery of iniquity." All Scripture tells us is that from somewhere in Satan's heart arose the simple but insidious idea: *I want something different from what God wants for my life.*

This battle of the wills was the basis of the first sin ever committed in the universe and of every sin since that time. At the root of every act of disobedience in your life is a conscious decision to place your desire above God's desire.

I know this next statement may offend some, but I want you to seriously consider it before rejecting it. Whenever you ask yourself, *What do I really want in life?* you are in danger of making the same mistake that led to Satan's eventual removal from heaven. I realize this cuts against the grain of what we often hear about dreaming, vision-casting, and goal-setting. "If you want a different life from the one you're living," some assert, "the first step is to close your eyes and imagine:

- the income you would like to earn
- the house you would like to own
- the automobile you would like to drive
- the work you would like to perform
- the kind of mate you would like to marry."

But if we acknowledge that God is our Creator and we are His creatures, then our first question should not be *What do I desire?* but *What does God desire for me?*

I realize that sometimes God reveals His will through our desires. The Bible says, "Delight yourself in the LORD; and He will give you the desires of your heart" (Psalm 37:4). If I am living in obedience to God, He can reveal His plan for my life through my desires.

Nevertheless, within the hidden corners of our hearts a desire lurks for something contrary to God's will for our lives. Just as Satan encouraged the kings of Babylon and Tyre to pursue that desire, the Tempter whispers to us, "There is a better way than God's way."

Satan's Plan B

As a result of Satan's misguided vision-casting about his future, God tossed him out of heaven along with an undetermined number of renegade angels who had decided they, too, were sick and tired of living under the tyranny of the Almighty. I think of a scene from the movie *Jerry Maguire* in which a highly successful sports agent played by Tom Cruise decides to form his own agency. After an impassioned plea to his fellow agents, he invites anyone and everyone who wants to build a better company on loftier principles to leave with him. Only one mousy secretary responds to the invitation. Once they're out the door, they suddenly realize they're on their own. No more salary, health insurance, or any other benefits. She looks at him as if to say, *"What do we do now, Einstein?"*

Satan fared a little better than Jerry Maguire. By some accounts as many as one-third of the angels chose to follow him in starting a new kingdom. Nevertheless, that means for every angel who said yes to Satan, two said no. The realization of the heavenly perks he and his followers had surrendered must have hit them as soon as they hit planet Earth. These fallen angels probably asked their leader, "What are we going to do now, Boss?"

A lethal mix of bitterness and desperation must have led Satan to declare to his dispirited troops, "The dream lives on! We will build a kingdom greater than God's. We will rule over the universe!"

Satan was correct in one way. The dream of building a rival kingdom that will one day dethrone God is still alive in the hearts of Satan and his followers. He is attempting to establish a shadow empire founded on the lie that life apart from God is both possible and preferable. He is actively recruiting as many as he can to join him in his misguided efforts.

Some might wonder, *Doesn't Satan realize that he cannot possibly succeed in his plan?* The possibility for self-delusion is limitless, especially when one is desperate. I saw a CNN documentary a few years ago about a famous evangelist who had been caught engaging in adulterous conduct. At the height of his popularity, his church was attracting five thousand people a week, and his ministry was receiving over a million dollars a day in contributions. His television program was seen on hundreds of stations around the world.

His ministry was destroyed after having his liaisons with prostitutes exposed and admitting to them. The documentary detailed his determination to rebuild his empire. Today, instead of five thousand a Sunday, only a few hundred attend. His ministry income has been reduced to a trickle of what it had been, and his television exposure is limited to a few cable outlets. Nevertheless, the evangelist is convinced that the sun will rise again on his religious kingdom.

Satan shares the same optimism about the future of his own empire. Although Satan is not omniscient and therefore cannot see the future as God can, he is thoroughly acquainted with the Bible (more so than many Christians). He knew of God's plan to send His Son to redeem mankind. He was aware of Jesus's claim that He would rise again from the dead. Satan is cognizant of God's intention to break his stranglehold on the earth and dispatch him into the lake of fire forever.

But Satan has never believed God would actually succeed in His plan, just as many of us don't really believe that we're going to die and stand before God to give an account of our lives. After all, if we *really* believed that, wouldn't we live differently?

Satan's desperation to regain his former glory and his doubt about God's ability to reclaim all that was lost through mankind's rebellion have led Satan to launch a full-scale assault on God's kingdom. This is being played out in three rounds.

Round 1: Deception

Perhaps Satan and his followers crash-landed on planet Earth just in time to see God's crowning work of creation.

> Then God said, "Let Us make man in Our image, according to Our likeness; and let them rule over the fish of the sea and over the birds of the sky and over the cattle and over all the earth, and over every creeping thing that creeps on the earth." God created man in His own image, in the image of God He created him; male and female He created them…. God saw all that He had made, and behold, it was very good. (Genesis 1:26–27, 31)

If you resented God as much as Satan did, the only thing worse than one God would be lots of little sons of God—or at least creatures who closely resembled Him—running around everywhere. Observing the Father's understandable pride over His new offspring, Satan must have entertained several sinister thoughts:

What if I were able to transform these human beings from God's servants into my slaves?

What if I were able to persuade them to join me in destroying their Father's kingdom?

What if I were able to turn God's grandest creation into his greatest mistake?

So the Garden of Eden became ground zero for the universal war between God and Satan. Through a scheme I will describe in greater detail later, Satan was able to persuade the first couple to follow him rather than obey God. By their decision, Adam and Eve not only became Satan's slaves, but they ensured that all subsequent generations were automatically born into satanic servitude. The apostle Paul describes the far-reaching effects of Adam's one fatal decision in his letter to the Romans.

> Therefore,…through one man sin entered into the world, and death
> through sin, and so death spread to all men, because all sinned.
> (Romans 5:12)

We will leave it to the theologians to debate how we are culpable for Adam's sin. Whether it is because we were genetically present in Adam when he sinned or because Adam was casting his vote for the entire human race when he rebelled is really immaterial. The result of Adam's choice is that all of humanity suddenly became part of Satan's empire.

The Creator could have understandably pouted over His creatures' fickleness, abandoned them to their deserved fate, and embarked on creating a new kind of companion. God certainly would have been justified in allowing Adam and his sin-infected offspring to remain prisoners of Satan forever. But He didn't. When God saw the desperate condition into which His creatures had fallen, something deep within God's heart was stirred with compassion. God's inexplicable and undeserved love for each one of His creatures moved Him to instigate a rescue plan.

But God, being rich in mercy, because of His great love with which He loved us, even when we were dead in our transgressions, made us alive together with Christ (by grace you have been saved). (Ephesians 2:4–5)

Round 2: Deliverance

November 27, 2003, will be a most unforgettable Thanksgiving Day for six hundred soldiers who were stationed in Baghdad. Early that morning the soldiers were ordered to assemble in a makeshift mess hall at Baghdad International Airport. Little did they know the elaborate preparations that had been unfolding during the preceding fifteen hours halfway around the world.

The president of the United States had left his ranch in Crawford, Texas, in an unmarked car a little after 7:00 p.m. the day before. Only a handful of people knew what the commander in chief planned. Once he arrived at the airport north of Waco, he boarded Air Force One for an all-night flight to Iraq. He would be in the first president in United States history to visit that country.

Because of the threat of missile attack, when the president's plane approached the airport, all interior lights were turned off, and the window shades were pulled down. The jetliner made a steep, quick, corkscrew descent in order to avoid possible enemy fire.

Meanwhile, in the mess hall at the airport, the troops had gathered for what they thought would be a speech by Paul Bremer, chief U.S. administrator in Iraq. Bremer stood at the podium and said he would like to read a proclamation from the president of the United States. He then paused and said it was customary for the most senior official present to read the president's words. "Is there anybody back there who's more senior than I?" Bremer asked.

On cue, President Bush emerged from behind the curtain as cheering soldiers climbed on chairs and tables to yell their approval. The surprise visit not only brought accolades from the battle-weary soldiers but also stunned the media and the world. Even the president's parents, who had been expecting him at the Thanksgiving table back in Crawford, were surprised. When asked by the media why he went to such great lengths to make the long journey to Iraq to visit the soldiers, the president responded, "It's got to be lonely for them. I thought it was important to send that message that we care for them."[3]

In spite of Adam and Eve's initial rebellion and their offspring's continued rebellion through the succeeding generations, God has never given up on the human race. Through miracles and messages, God has consistently communicated His love for His creatures.

But two thousand years ago, God did the unthinkable. In an elaborate scheme that had been devised before the beginning of the world (remember, man's rebellion did not take the omniscient God by surprise), the Creator took on human form, left the comfort of heaven, and came to this war-torn planet that was firmly in Satan's grip.

But God's visit to Earth differed from the president's visit to Iraq in two significant ways. First, the president's trip was planned so as to avoid his death. No temporary morale boost for the troops would be worth the loss of their commander. God's visit to Earth was planned so that He would experience death. Jesus's death on the cross was no accident; it was part of God's plan from the beginning of time. The apostle Peter, addressing the same crowd that had crucified Christ a few weeks earlier, declared that their murderous actions were all part of God's eternal purpose:

> This Man [Jesus], delivered over by the *predetermined plan and fore-knowledge of God*, you nailed to a cross by the hands of godless men and put Him to death. (Acts 2:23)

What would cause God to plan the excruciating torture and death of His own Son? That answer leads to a second difference between the president's trip to Iraq and Jesus's journey to the cross. The president came to *reassure* the troops; Jesus came to *rescue* the troops. The apostle Paul describes Christ's mission this way:

For He [the Father] rescued us from the domain of darkness, and transferred us to the kingdom of His beloved Son, in whom we have
redemption, the forgiveness of sins. (Colossians 1:13–14)

Before Jesus's sacrificial death on the cross, we were held hostage in Satan's
domain of darkness. We had "no hope" and we were "without God in the
world," as Paul wrote in Ephesians 2:12. But through His death, Jesus paid the
necessary price to redeem us from Satan's kingdom. The word *redeem* refers to
the purchasing of a slave, not setting him free. If you lived in Paul's day and
wanted to acquire a slave for your household, you would go to the marketplace
where slaves were displayed. When you found a slave that met your needs, you
would pay the asking price and the ownership of the slave was transferred to
you. The slave was not redeemed and then set free. Redemption simply
resulted in a change of masters.

Similarly, God has paid the necessary price in order to transfer you from
Satan's empire to God's empire. Choosing to accept God's offer of redemption
does not result in your serving no master but simply serving a new, more
benevolent Master. "You are not your own…for you have been bought with a
price," Paul reminds us in 1 Corinthians 6:19–20. Satan, fully aware of God's
desire to free as many of Satan's captives as possible, tried to thwart God's plan
of redemption from the moment Jesus Christ was conceived in Mary's womb.
Satan attempted to incite Joseph to divorce Mary for adultery, which could
have resulted in her death as well as the death of the Child she carried.

When that didn't work, Satan persuaded King Herod to try to kill the
Child by ordering the murder of every Hebrew male less than two years of age.

When that plan failed, Satan endeavored to entice Jesus to sin and therefore disqualify Himself as the spotless Lamb of God who could take away the
sins of the world.

When Jesus resisted Satan's overtures, the Enemy then encouraged the
religious leaders to murder Jesus prematurely before He fulfilled the necessary
prophecies concerning His death. But when the Lord cried out "It is finished"

that afternoon and rose from the grave three days later, Satan's vise grip on God's creation and His creatures was forever broken. Easter Sunday represents V-E Day for God and His creation.

> When [God] had disarmed the rulers and authorities, He made a public display of them, having triumphed over them through [Christ].
> (Colossians 2:15)

Yet, Satan's dream lives on. He continues to pursue the possibility of toppling God's kingdom by thwarting God's purposes.

Round 3: Desperation

Pick up the newspaper, observe the lives of your friends and family members, or simply examine the struggles within your own heart, and it's difficult to believe that Satan has really been defeated. As a book title claimed years ago, *Satan Is Alive and Well on Planet Earth*. In truth, he is not all that well. He suffered a mortal wound at the Cross that broke his power over God's creation. The date of his final judgment has already been set on God's calendar. The apostle John was given a sneak preview of Satan's end:

> And the devil who deceived them was thrown into the lake of fire and brimstone, where the beast and the false prophet are also; and they will be tormented day and night forever and ever. (Revelation 20:10)

Right now, we who are living in the time between Satan's initial disarming at the Cross and his ultimate destruction in the lake of fire are witnesses to (and sometimes victims of) his last acts of desperation. Whether or not he really believes he can alter his determined fate is unknown. What is clear is this: between now and his final judgment, Satan is determined to launch one final assault on God's kingdom.

Some believe that this final conflict will take place at the Battle of

Armageddon at the end of the Tribulation described in John's Revelation, chapters 16–19. Others place it after the thousand-year reign of Christ when Satan is given one last chance to deceive the world (see Revelation 20:7–9). Regardless of your view of the end times, what is evident is that Satan is marshaling as many troops as possible to wage this one last battle.

What is his game plan?

First, he wants to prevent those who are already enslaved to him from defecting to God's kingdom. Satan will do everything within his ability to prevent unbelievers from accepting God's offer of redemption through Christ. Even though the offer has been made to everyone, the Bible tells us that "the god of this world has blinded the minds of the unbelieving so that they might not see the light of the gospel of the glory of Christ, who is the image of God" (2 Corinthians 4:4).

Second, Satan has not given up on those of us who have gone over to God's side. Even though we now serve a new Master, Satan tries to persuade us that we are still under his control. If he can convince us that we have no choice but to obey his commands, then he can rob us of our birthright in Christ:

- the joy that comes from fellowship with God
- the benefits that accrue in this life from following God
- the influence we have to enlarge the kingdom of God
- the eternal rewards that can be ours for obedience to God

No wonder Jesus refers to Satan as a thief who comes only to "steal and kill and destroy" (John 10:10). But if Satan has been disarmed, how does he exercise so much influence over Christians and non-Christians alike? The answer to that question is the focus of the next chapter.

BLUEPRINT FOR YOUR DESTRUCTION

Satan's threefold plan for ruining your life

> Anyone who is not aware of a fight and a conflict in a
> spiritual sense is in a drugged and hazardous condition.
> —DAVID MARTYN LLOYD-JONES

You may not recall the name Mohammed Saeed Sahhaf, but you might remember him by his nickname, Baghdad Bob. He was Iraq's so-called minister of information during the final days before American forces captured the city of Baghdad in the spring of 2003. In spite of all evidence to the contrary, Baghdad Bob kept insisting that Iraq's brutal dictator Saddam Hussein was winning the conflict. On April 6, after coalition forces had secured Baghdad's Saddam International Airport and renamed it Baghdad International Airport, this minister of "disinformation" claimed, "We butchered the [enemy] force present at the airport."[1]

The following day, after U.S. troops marched through the center of Baghdad and stormed one of Saddam's palaces, Baghdad Bob declared, "There is no presence of the American columns in the city of Baghdad at all.... We besieged them and we killed most of them."[2] His comical efforts to deny what was visible to all became the fodder of late-night talk-show hosts. When the president of the United States was asked about him, he chuckled and said, "He's quite a guy, isn't he?"

Satan is a lot like Baghdad Bob. Although he was soundly defeated at the cross of Jesus Christ and the date of his final judgment is already on God's calendar, he attempts to persuade those who don't know any better that he is still in control. But unlike Baghdad Bob, there is nothing funny about Satan's lies. His ability to blind unbelievers to the freedom Christ offers results in their eternal separation from God in hell. But non-Christians are not the only ones who are victims of his propaganda. Many believers, unaware of Satan's disarmament at the Cross, still act as if he is their master.

They cower in fear at his threats.

They surrender to his temptations.

They allow themselves to be used for his purposes.

The result? Even if Satan cannot rob them of a place in heaven in the next life, he is able to deprive them of the benefits of being a child of God in this life. In the process, he is able to use them as accomplices in his ongoing assault on the kingdom of God.

Let's no longer talk about *them*. Let's talk about you for a moment. Do you realize *you* have an enemy who is determined to deceive you about his power (or lack thereof), deprive you of your privileges as a child of God, destroy your effectiveness as a servant of God, and deny you the rewards that God wants one day to bestow on you in heaven?

In addition to such devious objectives, Satan has also developed a detailed, personalized game plan to accomplish those goals in your life. That sobering truth is what prompted Paul to exhort the Christians at Ephesus to "put on the full armor of God, so that you will be able to stand firm against the schemes of the devil" (Ephesians 6:11).

The word "schemes" (*methodia* in Greek) was originally used to describe a wild animal that would methodically stalk and then suddenly attack its victim. The predator would not treat all its prey in the same way. Different prey required different strategies. In the same way, Satan has developed a unique plan for destroying your relationship with God, dividing your family, and diminishing your effectiveness as a witness for Christ. Think of it. Right now in the pit of hell, there is a completed blueprint with your name on it that details Satan's plan for robbing you of every good thing God has planned for you. Pastor Stu Weber wonders if you've considered this:

> Christian soldier, have you ever thought about yourself as a target of
> such strategies? Have you ever thought about your own picture and vital
> statistics sitting on a table in the war room of some demonic gathering?
>
> It isn't fantasy, my friend. It's solemn truth. You do have an
> enemy—one who employs battle strategies and tactics to bring about
> your destruction.[3]

If you're going to be successful in repelling the attacks of your enemy, you must realize Satan hates you and has a terrible plan for your life. While his blueprint for your demise is highly personalized, it usually involves one or more of the following three strategies.

Satan's Strategy No. 1: To Discourage You from Worshiping God

A few months ago at our annual Stump the Pastor session, during which our church members can ask me anything they desire, a little boy posed this question: "Why did God create Satan if He knew all the trouble he would cause?"

That's a good question, wouldn't you admit?

My usual reply to such difficult questions is, "It's a mystery of God" (which sounds much better than "I don't have a clue"). Fortunately, someone much wiser than I has provided me with needed insight into that mystery.

> Our God was neither surprised nor astonished [by Satan's rebellion], for
> of course He knew before it happened that it would happen, and He
> had His perfect plan ready to be put into effect. Although the Lord had
> the power to destroy Satan with a breath, He did not do so. It was as

though an edict had been proclaimed in heaven. "We shall give this rebellion a thorough trial. We shall permit it to run its full course. The universe shall see what a mere creature, though he be the highest creature ever to spring from God's Word, can do apart from Him. We shall watch this experiment and permit the universe of creatures to watch it, during this brief interlude between eternity past and eternity future called time. In the spirit of independence it shall be allowed to expand to its full extent. And the wreck and ruin which shall result will demonstrate to the universe, and forever, that there is no life, no joy, no peace apart from a complete dependence upon the Most High God, possessor of heaven and earth."[4]

You and I are part of an unfolding drama on the stage called planet Earth. The audience for this production is the universe of creatures in heaven (and probably hell) who are carefully watching to see how God deals with the rebellion of one of His creatures. The purpose of this ultimate reality show is not entertainment but a demonstration of God's power and character to that vast unseen audience of His created beings. This production will answer some important questions:

- Will God tolerate the revolt of His creatures?
- Does God love or hate those humans whom He created in His image?
- Is God justified in His eternal condemnation of those who fail to trust in Christ?
- Can God be trusted to keep His promises?
- Who is the better master to serve: God or Satan?

Satan is fully aware of the vast, unseen audience as well. Since he is filled with pride—the primary flaw that caused his expulsion from heaven—he is determined to redeem his reputation in the universe by discrediting God's character. If he cannot be successful in possessing the souls of God's redeemed creatures for all eternity, the next best thing is to turn them against God in this life and humiliate God as the heavenly audience watches.

How does Satan accomplish that goal? His primary tool is discouragement. Bill Anderton tells the story about the day the devil decided to go out of business. He conducted a sale in which his tools would be sold to whoever would pay the price.

> On the night of the sale, [the devil's tools] were all attractively displayed. Malice, hate, envy, jealousy, greed, sensuality, and deceit were among them. To the side lay a harmless wedge-shaped tool, which had been used much more than any of the rest.
>
> Someone asked the devil, "What's that? It's priced so high."
>
> The devil answered, "That's discouragement."
>
> "But why is it priced so much higher than [all the other tools]?" the onlooker persisted.
>
> "Because," replied the devil, "with that tool I can pry open and get inside a person's consciousness when I couldn't get near him with any of the others. Once discouragement gets inside, I can let all the other tools do their work."[5]

Discouragement was Satan's primary strategy against God's servant Job. As the Scottish preacher Alexander Whyte observed, "Till Christ came, no soul was ever made such a battleground between heaven and earth as Job's soul was made."[6] In the opening verses of Job's story we find this description of God's faithful servant:

> There was a man in the land of Uz whose name was Job; and that man was blameless, upright, fearing God and turning away from evil. (Job 1:1)

Meanwhile, in heaven, the drama behind the drama was unfolding. God, pointing to Earth, directed Satan's attention to the main character on stage:

> Have you considered My servant Job? For there is no one like him on the earth, a blameless and upright man, fearing God and turning away from evil. (Job 1:8)

In effect, God was saying to His adversary, "Not everyone has chosen to follow you, Satan. Here's just one example of a creature who loves Me and has chosen to serve Me."

But Satan was not about to allow God to have the last word. "Of course Job serves you," he essentially said. "Look at all the gifts you've bribed him with. He would be a fool not to follow you. But take away the gifts, and you will take away his allegiance to you."

God was convinced that Satan was wrong. But what about the other heavenly creatures who heard Satan's challenge? Maybe they weren't quite as certain: would God's crowning work of creation remain loyal if God removed the blessings? God made a decision to grant Satan limited permission to attack Job.

> Then the LORD said to Satan, "Behold, all that he has is in your power, only do not put forth your hand on him." So Satan departed from the presence of the LORD. (Job 1:12)

The remainder of the first two chapters of Job describes Satan's relentless assault on Job's possessions, family, and health. As Job sat on the ash heap of his incinerated possessions, his dead children, and his broken health, his wife asked, "Do you still hold fast your integrity? Curse God and die!" (Job 2:9).

That was Satan's goal! He wanted to discredit God to the entire universe. By so discouraging one of God's creatures, Satan imagined the creature would conclude that the Creator was not worthy of worship.

Satan employs the same strategy today. God granted Satan and his forces (the demons) limited power so they are able to use governing authorities, natural calamities, physical illnesses, and even other Christians to bring disaster and discouragement into our lives. What is his objective? To turn you against God and, in the process, dishonor God's reputation before all of His creation.

However, Satan's power to discourage us is not unlimited. Just as God prohibited Satan from killing Job (although I'm confident there were times Job wished such a restraint would have been removed), God has limited the devil's ability to hurt you. Martin Luther observed that the devil is God's devil. Satan has been compared to a junkyard dog on a very long leash. Although his power to destroy is considerable, it's also limited.

But why would God grant Satan even limited permission to discourage us? Doesn't that unnecessarily jeopardize God's reputation in the universe? What if significant numbers of us chose to abandon our fidelity to the Creator?

Untested faith is really no faith. Even Satan understands this principle. Job's profession of love for God meant little until it was placed in the crucible of trials. But when Satan had hit Job as hard as he possibly could, this servant of the Most High God cried out, "Though He slay me, I will hope in Him" (Job 13:15). I imagine at that moment the heavenly audience gasped in amazement not only at a creature who could endure such pain but at a God who could command such devotion.

This same drama continues to be played out at this very moment. Job has exited the stage, and it is now your turn to play your assigned part. The heavenly audience watches and wonders if Satan will be successful in breaking your allegiance to God. Will financial pressure, family conflicts, health issues, or the death of a loved one be enough to turn you away from God?

Whenever I think about Satan's strategy of discouragement, I am reminded of the testimony of the late Christian writer Joe Bayly who suffered the loss of three of his children. For many Christians, that would be enough to give up on God, but not for Joe Bayly. When asked how he was able to reconcile his faith in God with such suffering, he said, "We can go one of two directions when we can't reconcile a loss with our faith in God. Either we give up that faith in God, or we realize that He's in control and working out a plan, even though in the darkness we cannot see what the plan is. Faith means something when it is exercised in darkness."[7]

Satan's Strategy No. 2: To Distract You from Serving God

If Satan cannot persuade you to reject God, the next best thing is to distract you so you ignore God. The Adversary's goal is to create as much distance as possible between you and your Creator. In *The Screwtape Letters,* C. S. Lewis illustrates this tactic through a senior demon, Uncle Screwtape, who advises his novice nephew how to wage war against the "Enemy" (God).

> Like all young tempters, you are anxious to be able to report spectacular wickedness. But do remember, the only thing that matters is the extent to which you separate the man from the Enemy. It does not matter how small the sins are, provided that their cumulative effect is to edge the man away from the Light and out into the Nothing. Murder is no better than cards if cards can do the trick. Indeed, the safest road to Hell is the gradual one—the gentle slope, soft underfoot, without sudden turnings, without signposts.[8]

While fostering overt disobedience is one way to create a wedge between God and us, Satan does not always have to resort to such obvious strategies. Many times he can achieve the same result simply by distracting us from our relationship with God through what a previous generation of Christians called worldliness.

The term *worldliness* is sometimes associated with those dour-looking Christians of yesteryear who peered disapprovingly down their long noses at people who danced, went to movies, or wore two-piece swimsuits. Such people were labeled worldly and treated with the highest degree of disdain. I am using the term *worldliness*, however, to refer to a preoccupation with the delights and details of living in this world. Such a preoccupation might manifest itself in various ways:

- You choose to watch ESPN *SportsCenter* every night instead of reading your Bible.
- You allow the ups and downs of the stock market to determine your emotional well-being.
- You permit concerns about your child's social standing at school to fill your mind during the Sunday morning worship service.
- You become so consumed with your job that you feel you can't be involved in any meaningful ministry.

Perhaps a little confession time is in order here. As I write these words about the distractions of worldliness, I am having difficulty concentrating because of a breaking news story that tempts me to click on the CNN Web site every few moments. While there is nothing sinful about checking the news, it becomes a problem when it interferes with my assigned task in this war against Satan. It is that kind of interference Paul had in mind when he reminded Timothy that "no soldier in active service entangles himself in the affairs of everyday life, so that he may please the one who enlisted him as a soldier" (2 Timothy 2:4).

Notice that Paul did not say "no soldier in active service *involves* himself in the affairs of everyday life." Even soldiers have to give some attention to the mundane details of living such as eating, sleeping, paying bills, and cleaning the house.

We make a serious mistake when we assume that these daily duties are always at odds with God's purpose for our lives. Many times the primary ways we serve the One who "enlisted" us are through the jobs He has gifted us to perform, the children He has blessed us to rear, the family and friends He has given us to love, and the myriad of details those responsibilities involve. What Paul is warning against is allowing the pressures and pleasures of those responsibilities to interfere with our God-given purpose in life.

Jesus described the dangers of that kind of preoccupation in His parable about the soils, recorded in Luke 8:4–15. Jesus used an agricultural analogy to answer the question, "Why doesn't everyone who hears God's Word respond in the same way?" Jesus explained that different reactions to God's Word are due to different conditions of the human heart, as represented by the different types of soil on which seed (representing God's Word) falls.

Occasionally God's Word falls on a heart that is so hardened by constant rejection of the truth that it cannot be penetrated. Other times, Jesus said, the seed falls on shallow soil that has a bed of limestone underneath it, preventing the new plant from developing a root system. When the hot, Palestinian sun begins to shine on the plant, it withers away because it cannot go deep into the ground and gain the moisture it needs. This soil represents the person who initially receives God's Word with enthusiasm but never develops a spiritual root system that allows him to grow in faith. When the scorching heat of trial begins to beat on his life, his faith withers away.

The third condition of the human heart Jesus described is the one that is relevant to our discussion about distractions.

> The seed which fell among the thorns, these are the ones who have
> heard, and as they go on their way they are choked with worries and
> riches and pleasures of this life, and bring no fruit to maturity. (verse 14)

In this instance, the seed penetrates the soil, develops a root system, and even begins to bear fruit. However, in the soil is a vast network of weeds that has been there for years. Slowly, the weeds grow too and wrap themselves around the new plants, gradually strangling the life out of them. Jesus describes three varieties of spiritual weeds that can entangle our hearts and choke out our desire for God.

Worries

Someone has described worry as a thin stream of fear trickling through the mind. If encouraged, it cuts a channel into which all other thoughts are drained. Have you ever been enjoying a day of relaxation with your family, working diligently on a project at work, or spending some time alone with God when out of nowhere an alien and troublesome thought enters your mind that begins *what if*?

What if I'm terminated from my job?

What if my mate leaves me?

What if I develop a serious illness?

The more you attempt to dismiss this unwanted and unwarranted fear, the more you find yourself obsessing over it. You are paralyzed by what has now become a fixation. You can't enjoy your family, you can't perform your assigned tasks, and you have no desire to spend time with God.

Where does such debilitating fear originate? Not from God. "For God has not given us a spirit of timidity, but of power and love and discipline" (2 Timothy 1:7). If fear does not originate from God, then with whom does it originate?

Here's a clue. Have you ever discovered that most of the things you worry about never transpire? One study I read claimed that 92 percent of the things we worry about have little to no chance of occurring. Most of the fears that invade our lives are unfounded. They are based on lies. The father of all fabrications is Satan, whom Jesus described as "a liar and the father of lies" (John 8:44).

Riches

At first glance, you may feel you can skip this section if you don't have a six-figure income or a seven-figure net worth. Yet, compared to the rest of the world, you are wealthy if you have a roof over your head, more than two or three changes of clothes, and a good idea of where your next meal is coming from.

But even if you do not accept the notion of your relative wealth, you can still have your love for God strangled by money. Those who consider themselves poor are in just as much danger of worshiping money as those who are wealthy. Most of us are aware of Jesus's statement: "You cannot serve both God and money" (Matthew 6:24, NLT). But few people are aware of the verse that follows this one:

> For this reason I say to you, do not be worried about your life, as to what you will eat or what you will drink; nor for your body, as to what you will put on. Is not life more than food, and the body more than clothing? (Matthew 6:25)

Jesus's warning against the love of money was addressed to those who were experiencing a lack, rather than an abundance, of financial resources. Feeding and clothing their families were their primary concerns. Believing that money was the key to their survival and future security, they allowed it to become the focus of their lives.

Two thousand years later, not much has changed. Most people are worried they have too little money, not that they have too much. The investment industry spends hundreds of millions of dollars every year reminding us of the pitfalls of potential poverty. We are warned that we need to accumulate at least one million dollars by the time we are sixty-five, or we'll be eating oatmeal in our twilight years. The insurance industry expends similar amounts to scare us into buying long-term nursing-home policies so our resources won't be depleted when we're elderly. Mutual-fund companies encourage us to set aside hundreds of dollars every month for our children's college education—even before our children are born—so that rising tuition costs won't bankrupt the family. While all this might be wise counsel, it is advice built on *fear,* the fear that we won't have enough resources to meet our future needs.

More than one hundred years ago, French historian Alexis de Tocqueville remarked that apart from the United States he knew of no other country "where the love of money has taken stronger hold on the affections of men."[9]

The Bible describes a preoccupation with finances as Spiritual Enemy #1 to our relationship with God:

> For the love of money is a root of all sorts of evil, and some by longing
> for it have wandered away from the faith and pierced themselves with
> many griefs. (1 Timothy 6:10)

Pleasures of this life

By referring to pleasures as a third potential distraction in our relationships with God, Jesus was not condemning any enjoyment of life. In fact, pleasure—kept in balance—can draw us closer to God, who is the Creator of all good things.

Satan, aware of pleasure's potential danger, tries to push us into one of two extremes when it comes to pleasure. One extreme is to deny ourselves completely of any enjoyment in life. We become convinced that reading a book just for the fun of it, watching a TV program or a movie, eating that favorite food (when it's not part of your diet), or purchasing that dress or shirt you don't really need are wastes of time and resources that could be devoted to more-spiritual pursuits.

In an attempt to enhance our relationship with God, we embark on a program of rigid self-discipline, denying ourselves any pleasure in life. By doing so, we are actually playing into the Enemy's plan. C. S. Lewis exposes that plan through the advice that the senior demon, Uncle Screwtape, offers his nephew:

> Never forget that when we are dealing with any pleasure in its healthy
> and normal and satisfying form, we are, in a sense, on the Enemy's
> [God's] ground. I know we have won many a soul through pleasure.
> All the same, it is His invention, not ours. He made the pleasures; all
> our research so far has not enabled us to produce one. All we can do is
> to encourage the humans to take the pleasures which our Enemy has
> produced, at times, or ways, or in degrees, which He has forbidden.[10]

However, if Satan cannot persuade us to abstain from pleasure, he will push us toward the other extreme: worshiping pleasure. The apostle Paul warned about those who have become "lovers of pleasure rather than lovers of God" (2 Timothy 3:4). We see evidence of the wild pursuit of pleasure all around us.

Today Americans spend more than five hundred billion dollars annually on recreational pursuits. Lake houses, out-of-town trips, and endless sports activities keep many families in perpetual motion, leaving them exhausted. They are always playing catch-up, so there is little time to nurture their relationships with God.

Even when we're not vacationing or enjoying recreation, we're working as hard as we possibly can so that one day we can entertain ourselves 24/7 during that utopian period of time known as retirement (a concept completely foreign to the Bible). As a pastor, I have seen many couples who have given up vital ministries when they reach that magical age. They believe they can shirk most of their responsibilities so they can travel around the country in a Winnebago with no greater concern than wondering how they will be entertained each day.

What is it that is distracting you from your relationship with God? Have the what-ifs of worry sapped your emotional strength? Has money—earning it, saving it, or spending it—become the focus of your life? Has the pursuit of pleasure become the grand obsession of your existence?

The first step in defeating the Enemy's plan is to recognize the specific strategy he is using to distract you from your relationship with God.

SATAN'S STRATEGY NO. 3: TO DECEIVE YOU INTO DISOBEYING

Discouragement and distraction represent the equally lethal, but admittedly more subtle, tactics Satan uses to separate believers from God. But overt disobedience to God's commands is Satan's preferred objective because of the resulting spiritual fallout in the Christian's life and the disillusionment such disobedience produces in others. I imagine you can immediately think of a Christian you deeply respected who, without any apparent warning, did one of the following:

- deserted his mate in the pursuit of someone more appealing
- allowed the allure of money to trap him into some illegal business scheme
- became ensnared in pornography or some other kind of sexual immorality

While such falls appear sudden, they rarely are. Consider a gigantic cliff of snow that without any apparent warning becomes a tremendous avalanche burying everything in its path. The avalanche is the result of slow, imperceptible changes in temperature and shiftings of weight that go unnoticed to the casual observer until it is too late.

In the same way, most of us do not fall into sin without warning. Overt disobedience is usually the result of a gradual change in our spiritual temperature and a shift in our priorities that one day results in a catastrophic calamity. But there is also an external force at work against us. We have an opponent who is looking for the opportune time to push us over the edge when we are most vulnerable. One popular Christian writer ponders a phone call he received informing him that a Christian leader had fallen into sexual immorality:

> Do you think that this man, a follower of Christ, in his heart of hearts really wanted to fall? What man begins his journey wishing, "I think one day, after twenty years of ministry, I'll torpedo the whole thing with an affair"? He was picked off; the whole thing was plotted.... He was set up for a fall. Unless you are aware that that's what it is, you'll be taken out, too.[11]

Since we do have an active adversary who is trying to take us out, we need to be aware of his methods for deceiving us into disobedience. The New Testament writer James exposes Satan's strategy with a simple formula:

> But each one is tempted when he is carried away and enticed by his own lust. (James 1:14)

Before we look at the formula itself, let's consider this word *tempted*. In the English language the word *tempt* means "to entice to do evil by promise of gain." Satan lures us to disobedience by dangling the proverbial carrot in front of us, just as he did with Eve in the garden (for Eve, a piece of fruit rather than a vegetable).

"Disobey God and your deepest desires will be fulfilled," Satan promised the first woman, just as he promises us today. What the Tempter fails to disclose with his offer is that instead of satisfying our cravings, sin only increases those cravings until we are consumed and destroyed by our own desires.

I once read an account of how Eskimos kill wolves. They take a knife blade and coat it with animal blood, allowing it to dry in the frigid temperature. Then they coat the knife with several more layers of blood until the blade is completely concealed. The knife is then placed upright in the frozen ground.

The wolf, attracted by the scent of the blood, starts licking the knife. He begins to lick faster and faster. So strong is his craving for the blood that he does not notice the razor-sharp sting on his tongue, nor does he recognize the moment when his insatiable hunger is being satisfied by his own warm blood. His appetite just craves more and more blood until the dawn finds him dead in the snow.

Disobedience always leads to death, whether it is the death of family, reputation, friendships, dreams, or relationship with God. But like the blood-coated knife blade, the destructive power of sin is often concealed inside an appealing temptation that Satan custom designs to satisfy our deepest yearning.

James uses a similar analogy to describe Satan's method of deception. To be "carried away" and "enticed" by our own lust is to be drawn toward a trap that is both appealing and lethal. The word picture James paints can also describe a fish so blinded by its own hunger that it snaps at the bait dangling in front of it. It does not see the concealed hook that will destroy it.

Satan, the expert hunter and the master fisherman, knows precisely how to draw us toward sin and destruction. Here's a formula that will help you remember James's insight about our enemy's methodology:

Corrupt Desires + Right Bait + Wrong Choice = Sin

Let's look at each of these factors in the temptation equation more carefully.

Corrupt Desires

The phrase "carried away," used by James, means "to be drawn by an inward power." Each of us possesses strong appetites that will draw us toward the trap Satan has set for us or the bait he drops in front of us. Those cravings include an insatiable desire for certain things:

- recognition
- emotional intimacy with others

- sexual fulfillment
- food and clothing
- power
- possessions

It's important to understand that there is nothing wrong with any of these desires. They are part of the basic wiring installed by our Creator. The problem is that our natural desires have been corrupted since the first couple's fall in the garden. Adam and Eve's attempt to satisfy their natural desires in their own way, rather than in God's way, has now become a part of our basic DNA. We easily fall victim to the same lie that Satan used with Eve: *God's commands are designed to rob you of what you really desire in life.*

Sound familiar?

God's sex-in-marriage-only restriction will rob you of exhilarating sexual fulfillment.

God's commands to give generously will rob you of financial security.

God's instructions concerning humility and service will rob you of deserved recognition from others.

Having bought into Satan's lie that God cannot be trusted to provide what we need, and that we're responsible for our own well-being, we're perfectly set up for the next factor in the temptation equation.

Right Bait

Not long after I arrived at my present church, one of our older deacons invited me to go fishing with him early one Saturday morning. I would just as soon have spent the morning in the dentist's chair. I have hated fishing ever since my first expedition as a little boy when I caught nothing except my friend's right eyebrow in my first attempt at casting. My morning excursion with my deacon friend yielded the same result. I sat there waiting for the slightest tug on my line while my companion pulled out one fish after another.

Finally, I had to ask, "Bob, why are you having so much better luck than I?"

The crusty old fisherman said, "Preacher, luck has nothing to do with it. First, if you're going to catch fish, you have to smell like a fish. This morning

I didn't shower, shave, or put on cologne or deodorant [a fact easily verifiable]. Second, you have to use the right bait. Different fish like different bait."

When James writes about our being "enticed" into temptation, he is using a fishing term that means "hooked." Satan, an expert fisherman, knows what bait to dangle in front of us. We don't all crave the same thing at the same time. Depending on our circumstances or season of life, we have varying appetites.

A rocky period in your marriage may cause you to crave sexual intimacy, so Satan dangles just the right *someone* in your life.

A missed promotion at work may cause you to hunger for recognition, so Satan dangles a possible job transfer that is outside of God's will for your life.

An unforeseen emergency may cause you to seek financial security, so Satan dangles a dishonest business deal before you.

Like any good fisherman, Satan not only knows what bait to drop in front of us, but when to drop it. Unlike God, Satan is not omniscient (all knowing). He can't read our minds, but then, he doesn't need to. By carefully observing life circumstances and studying our habits, he knows what bait to use and when to use it.

While all of us experience unique moments opportune for Satan's temptations, there are general times we are prone to snap at Satan's enticements.

1. **When you've just experienced great success.** Mountain climbers will tell you, as hard and grueling as hiking to the summit can be, it is the descent from the peak that poses the greatest threat. Why? After his achievement the climber faces an emotional letdown that can lead to carelessness. The apostle Paul warned about the vulnerability often accompanying victory: "Therefore let him who thinks he stands take heed that he does not fall" (1 Corinthians 10:12).

2. **When you're tired.** The legendary football coach Vince Lombardi observed that fatigue makes cowards of us all. I want to add that fatigue can also make *victims* of us all. After the prophet Elijah had run ninety miles to escape the threats of Jezebel, he crawled under a tree and asked

the Lord to take his life (see 1 Kings 18–19). For what other reason would a man who had just confronted and killed 850 false prophets, suddenly flee in fear of one disgruntled female? The emotional exhaustion of Elijah's confrontation with the prophets on Mount Carmel led to a distorted perspective about Jezebel's threats. The physical fatigue of running ninety miles led to physical exhaustion and depression. During these periods of emotional and physical depletion, we are particularly susceptible to the Enemy's lies.

3. **When you're alone.** The loneliness that accompanies an unexpected divorce, the painful death of a loved one, or just a business trip to a strange city for a few days can make you vulnerable to Satan's temptations. Satan whispers: "No one cares about you." "No one will ever know." "God has abandoned you." These are just some of the lies Satan whispers in our solitude. His purpose is to persuade us to disobey our Creator.

4. **When you're waiting on God.** Satan can gain a great advantage in your life during that seemingly endless period of time between your desperate cry for God's help and His ultimate answer. The Adversary argues, "Since God is either unaware of your need or really doesn't care about your situation, you'd better take matters into your own hands." Abraham fell for that line. Convinced that God was unwilling or unable to keep His promise of a child, the old patriarch and his wife decided twenty-five years of waiting on God was enough. Their plan to have Abraham father a child through their slave Hagar was a catastrophic mistake. It still reverberates throughout the entire world in the continuing Israeli-Arab conflict.

All four of the above factors described Jesus's circumstances when tempted by Satan in the wilderness. He'd just experienced a great spiritual victory at His baptism when God identified him as "My beloved Son, in whom I am well-pleased" (Matthew 3:17). He was no doubt spiritually exhausted from forty days of fasting. He was alone in the desert wilderness. He was waiting on God for the beginning of His ministry, which would culminate with His death on a cross, resurrection from the grave, and ascension into heaven. It was at this time, the gospel writers record, that the "tempter came" to Jesus (Matthew 4:3). Don't be surprised if it's at those same times he comes to you as well.

Wrong Choice

The third factor in the temptation equation is the most important and the one over which we exercise the most control: our choices. Our corrupted desires are not our fault. We can thank Adam and Eve for passing those along to us. We have no ability to control which bait Satan selects to drop in front of us. Unless we're willing to isolate ourselves from everyone and everything in life, some alluring enticements will eventually find their way into our lives. Remember, isolation did not prevent the Tempter from reaching Jesus.

We do have control over our responses to Satan's bait, however. Unfortunately, many Christians follow the advice of playwright Oscar Wilde on how to handle temptation: "The only way to get rid of temptation is to yield to it."[12]

Tragically, too many Christians assume that because they still possess desires that are contrary to God's will, they must yield to those desires. But Paul declares that the power of those desires, which he calls the old self, was crushed the moment we trusted in Christ as our Savior:

> Knowing this, that our old self was crucified with Him, in order that
> our body of sin might be done away with, so that we would no longer
> be slaves to sin; for he who has died is freed from sin. (Romans 6:6–7)

Speaking of traps, don't fall into the snare of equating temptation with sin. Some people mistakenly assume that craving something outside of God's will is tantamount to sin, and they feel needlessly guilty and defeated. If temptation is a sin, then Jesus was the greatest sinner of all time since He endured the greatest temptations ever known to man! What proved Jesus to be the blameless Son of God was not the absence of temptation in His life, but the absence of yielding to those temptations.

For we do not have a high priest who cannot sympathize with our
weaknesses, but One who has been tempted in all things as we are, yet
without sin. (Hebrews 4:15)

During the forty days Jesus spent alone in the wilderness, the devil pulled
out every lure he had in his tackle box of temptations. Satan offered to satisfy
the Lord's intense hunger apart from God; Jesus said no. Satan promised Jesus
an opportunity to rule over the kingdoms of the world without the suffering
of the cross; Jesus refused. Satan presented to Jesus a way to have what He
wanted without having to wait on God's timing; Jesus would not give in.

We are tempted to say, "Yes, but He was the Son of God. No wonder He
had such willpower!" Paul's central argument in Romans 6 is this: the same
power that raised Jesus from the grave is now at work in your life, giving you
the ability to say no to every temptation Satan throws your way.

Therefore we have been buried with Him through baptism into death,
so that as Christ was raised from the dead through the glory of the
Father, so we too might walk in newness of life. (Romans 6:4)

You don't have to become a casualty on the battlefield. You don't have to
be another notch on the Enemy's belt. You do have a choice.

Demons in the World Today

Satan's sidekicks are no laughing matter

> Demons are neither phony nor funny.
> —Charles R. Swindoll

Have you ever felt an inexplicable weight of emotional oppression? For no logical reason you felt depressed and could not shake that feeling no matter how hard you tried.

Have you ever engaged in an argument with another person that went further than either of you intended? Tempers flared hotter, and the words become more vindictive than the situation warranted? It was as if there were a third person in the room, egging on the conflict beyond reasonable boundaries.

Have you ever experienced one of those really productive days when you were rapidly crossing off items on your to-do list when suddenly an alien thought entered your mind that filled you with fear? As hard as you tried to think about something else, you were unable to rid yourself of the thought seizing control of your emotions.

Have you been ambushed by a temptation that seemed to come out of nowhere? If you didn't know better, you would believe that God brought this enticement into your life because it seemed so custom designed to your taste.

If you have experienced one or more of these situations, then you have come face to face with the world of demons. "Now, Robert, isn't that a little bit over the top?" you ask. "Aren't depression, anger, fear, and temptation the products of our fallen nature that you wrote about in the last chapter?" Not completely. The Bible does attribute many of our problems to the gravitational pull toward sin that resides within each of us: "But each one is tempted when he is carried away and enticed by his own lust" (James 1:14).

Without that inherited (as well as cultivated) taste for those things outside of God's will for our lives, we would never be tempted to grab the baited hook of immoral relationships, selfish agendas, and greed-based pursuits. Nevertheless, someone has to be choosing the specific bait that appeals to us and determining the right time to place it before us. Up to now, we have identified that someone as our adversary, Satan (the literal meaning of *Satan* is "adversary" or "opponent").

But as we saw in chapter 2, Satan is not God's equal. Unlike God, Satan has not always existed. He was created by God. As a creature, Satan does not possess the attributes of the Creator.

Satan does not possess unlimited knowledge.

Satan is not all powerful.

Satan is not able to be in more than one place at a time.

Passages in the Bible such as Job 1 indicate that Satan has access to heaven (but it is a limited-access pass) and that he rails against Christians hoping to change God's attitude toward us.

Just look at your so-called servant [your name here] and what he does when he thinks no one is watching, he says to God. *Do you really want someone like that up here with you forever? His presence would definitely damage property values around here. Why don't you let me take him where he really belongs?*

The apostle John, anticipating the time when Satan will be permanently banished from God's presence, described Satan's role as chief prosecutor against believers:

> For the *accuser of our brethren* has been thrown down, he who accuses
> them before our God day and night. (Revelation 12:10)

If the thought of having Satan pointing out 24/7 all your flaws before God and arguing why you belong in hell rather than heaven makes you a little nervous, realize that you have the best defense attorney money *can't* buy. His name is Jesus Christ, and He is seated at God's right hand reminding the Father of the price that has already been paid for your sins. The same apostle John who identifies our adversary also describes our advocate.

> And if anyone sins, we have an Advocate with the Father, Jesus
> Christ the righteous; and He Himself is the propitiation for our
> sins; and not for ours only, but also for those of the whole world.
> (1 John 2:1–2)

The word translated "Advocate" pictures a defense attorney who pleads his client's case before a jury. Since Jesus Christ is the One who "speaks…in our defense," as the New International Version says in 1 John, we do not need to worry about Satan's accusations.

But if the devil is busy in heaven accusing us, then he cannot also be on Earth tempting us since he is not omnipresent (present everywhere at once). On the rare occasions when he leaves heaven to bring heartache and destruction into the life of someone like Job, he is incapable of tempting someone else at the same time. That means Satan is not directly involved in tempting very many people. More than likely, he saves his road trips from heaven for special projects that warrant his personal attention.

So if Satan is not the one tempting us, who is? Fortunately for the devil, he does not have to be everywhere at once. He has an army of minions called demons to assist him in his plot to establish a rival kingdom.

THE TRUTH ABOUT DEMONS

If you're like most people, you're probably a little skeptical about the subject of demons. Like Satan, demons have been caricatured as comical figures sitting on our shoulders whispering sweet temptations into our ears. Others trivialize their existence by referring to "inner demons," as if these were nothing more than someone's less admirable impulses.

But a friend of mine assures us "demons are neither funny nor phony." The Bible teaches they are formidable spiritual forces under the Enemy's domain, intent on fulfilling their master's plans for our destruction. Look again at the seminal passage in the New Testament concerning spiritual warfare:

> Put on the full armor of God, so that you will be able to stand firm
> against the schemes of the devil. For our struggle is not against flesh
> and blood, but against the *rulers*, against the *powers*, against the world
> *forces* of this darkness, against the spiritual *forces* of wickedness in the
> heavenly places. (Ephesians 6:11–12)

The plural references to rulers, powers, and forces indicate Satan is not alone in his battle against believers. If Satan is the brain behind the operation, then demons are the brawn. They are the devil's foot soldiers who execute his plan. If, indeed, our primary struggle is against these demons, then it seems logical to gather as much intelligence possible about them as so we can successfully defeat them.

Demons in the Old Testament

Although there are admittedly few references to demons in the Old Testament, they are mentioned occasionally. Primarily, demons were unseen powers that induced the Israelites to worship false gods.

> They [the Israelites] sacrificed to demons who were not God,
> To gods whom they have not known,
> New gods who came lately,
> Whom your fathers did not dread. (Deuteronomy 32:17)

The goat demons mentioned in Leviticus 17:7 were references to goat-like idols that were rooted in demonic powers. When the Israelites embraced, rather than destroyed, the pagan gods of Canaan—and actually sacrificed their children to false deities such as Molech—the psalmist declares they were actually sacrificing "their sons and their daughters to the demons" (Psalm 106:37).

DEMONS IN THE NEW TESTAMENT

Every writer of the New Testament (except for the unknown author of Hebrews) refers to the existence of demons. There are more than one hundred different passages mentioning demons. The first book of the New Testament written, the book of James, teaches that demons are orthodox in their theology. "You believe that God is one. You do well; the demons also believe, and shudder" (James 2:19).

To be a Christian entails more than mere intellectual assent to the right set of beliefs. James, addressing a group of Jewish believers, revealed that demons accepted the most basic tenet of Judaism: the oneness of God. If James were writing to Gentile believers today, he might say, "You believe that Jesus is the Son of God. Great! The demons also believe that, and they shudder!"

It may surprise you to know that demons acknowledge Jesus Christ as the Savior of the world who died on the cross and rose again from the dead. In fact, they probably believe those truths more heartily than you or I do, since they were eyewitnesses to those historical events. It's not enough to believe that Jesus is the Savior of the world; I must trust in Him as *my* Savior. It is not sufficient to accept that He died for the sins of the world; I must believe He died for *my* sins.

Demons are also mentioned in the last book of the Bible. In Revelation, John describes how God will use demons to accomplish His purpose of gathering world forces together for the great final conflict known as Armageddon.

> And I saw coming out of the mouth of the dragon and out of the
> mouth of the beast and out of the mouth of the false prophet, three

unclean spirits like frogs; for they are spirits of *demons*, performing signs,
which go out to the kings of the whole world, to gather them together
for the war of the great day of God, the Almighty. (Revelation 16:13–14)

The majority of references to demons occur in the gospels, which detail
the life and ministry of Jesus Christ. You can understand why. The invasion of
planet Earth by the Son of God was intended to reclaim God's creation and
release Satan's captives. This so threatened the devil and his demons that they
unleashed their full arsenal against the divine Deliverer.

Later in this chapter we will examine the most famous encounter between
Jesus and demons, uncovering valuable insights about their personalities. Jesus
not only taught about demons, but actually interacted with them, proving
they are real beings rather than figments of someone's overactive imagination.

The Origin of Demons

Because the Bible does not explicitly tell us the origin of demons, some people have speculated they could be the spirits of non-Christians who have
passed away. Others trace their beginning to the immoral union of the "sons
of God" and the "daughters of men" described in Genesis 6. Some speculate
that demons represent the spirits of an entire race of people who preceded
Adam and Eve and were destroyed because of their rebellion against God.

The most logical (and I believe, biblical) explanation for the origin of
demons is that they were angels who chose to follow Lucifer in his rebellion
against God. I say "logical" because there is no specific passage in the Bible that
claims a group of angels were cast out of heaven along with Lucifer. You may
ask, "What about Revelation's citation of Satan's angels thrown down to earth?"

And the great dragon was thrown down, the serpent of old who is
called the devil and Satan, who deceives the whole world; he was
thrown down to the earth, and his angels were thrown down with him.
(Revelation 12:9)

These verses could be describing the past conflict in heaven between Lucifer and God. However, many scholars believe the context of this passage (midpoint during the Tribulation), points to some future event, not a past occurrence.

Regardless of when this event occurs, Revelation 12:9 reveals Satan has a group of helpers referred to as "angels," perhaps because of their origin. In other passages, Satan's minions are described as "demons" (Matthew 12:24). Since the Bible uses the terms *angels* and *demons* interchangeably to refer to Satan's helpers, it seems logical to assume they are one and the same. Not all angels are demons, but all demons were once angels.

THE PERSONALITY OF DEMONS

Demons represent the "spiritual forces of wickedness" (see Ephesians 6:12) that are aligned against us. But they're more than just forces or concepts. They're actual beings who possess many of the same attributes we do. Look at one of many encounters Jesus had with the demonic world:

> And when He came out onto the land, He was met by a man from the city who was possessed with demons; and who had not put on any clothing for a long time, and was not living in a house, but in the tombs. Seeing Jesus, he cried out and fell before Him, and said in a loud voice, "What business do we have with each other, Jesus, Son of the Most High God? I beg You, do not torment me."… They were imploring Him not to command them to go away into the abyss.
>
> Now there was a herd of many swine feeding there on the mountain; and the demons implored Him to permit them to enter the swine. And He gave them permission. And the demons came out from the man and entered the swine; and the herd rushed down the steep bank into the lake and was drowned. (Luke 8:27–28, 31–33)

Who was this man who was possessed by a multitude of demons? What did this man do to cause these evil spirits to feel at home in his body? Is it possible for Christians to be controlled by demons? We will save the "can Christians be demon-possessed" discussion for the next section.

However, instead of focusing on the man himself, look at the personality of these demonic forces who had seized control of this individual.

First, demons possess *intelligence*. They are aware of what is happening around them. They instantly recognized Jesus as the Son of the Most High God.

Second, demons experience *emotions*. In this case they demonstrated fear that Jesus would cast them out of the man and into the abyss (verse 31), a term the Bible uses to describe a place of confinement for demons.

Third, demons have *wills*. Unlike inanimate objects, such as the book you are holding or the chair in which you are sitting, demons have desires upon which they act. In this case, they begged Jesus not to cast them into the abyss, offered Jesus an alternative plan, then submitted themselves to His command.

Fourth, demons have *names*. According to verse 30, the chief demon taking control of this man was named Legion, a military term referring to three thousand to six thousand soldiers.

Demons possess all the attributes you possess: intelligence, emotion, a will, and a name. The fact that Jesus actually carried on a conversation with demonic spirits, and took action against them, is convincing evidence they are real beings rather than crude attempts by first-century writers to communicate the concept of evil.

Demons and Unbelievers

Since demons are under the authority of Satan ("the devil and his angels," Matthew 25:41), it only makes sense that their purpose be in alignment with Satan's purpose. They assist him in building a shadow kingdom that rivals, and they hope will one day topple, God's kingdom. They are responsible for executing Satan's carefully conceived schemes involving both unbelievers and believers.

Demons work overtime to blind non-Christians to the liberating truth of the gospel in order to keep them in bondage to Satan. However, knowing the religious bent that even unbelievers retain as a result of being created in God's image, the Enemy tries to redirect a non-Christian's desire to worship away from Jesus Christ. The Old Testament attributes the enticement to worship false gods as originating with demons. Whether those false gods are named Baal, Asherah, Mohammed, Buddha, or Confucius, they are part of Satan's scheme to keep people from discovering God's exclusive way to heaven through Jesus Christ.

Just a few moments ago I received an e-mail from our associate pastor who is leading 108 people from our congregation on a mission trip to Africa. He wrote about one of our members who attempted to share the gospel with an African woman deeply involved in witchcraft. The African abruptly cut off the visitor and said, "The spirits will not allow me to trust in Christ."

But counterfeit religions that bind and blind unbelievers so they cannot accept Christ are not limited to third-world countries. Demons also inspire religious systems in our own culture, systems that have respectable denominational titles attached to them. False teaching that blinds people to the gospel may be wrapped in fine clerical robes and be articulated through the voices of educated and refined ministers. Don't be fooled. If any teaching contradicts the biblical message that salvation is through faith in Jesus Christ alone, that religious system is demonically inspired.

"Aren't you being overly harsh?" you may ask. No more so than the apostle John.

> Beloved, do not believe every spirit, but test the spirits to see whether they are from God, because many false prophets have gone out into the world. By this you know the Spirit of God: every spirit that confesses that Jesus Christ has come in the flesh is from God; and every spirit that does not confess Jesus is not from God; this is the *spirit of the antichrist*, of which you have heard that it is coming, and now it is already in the world.... By this we know the spirit of truth and the spirit of error. (1 John 4:1–3, 6)

Any religion, regardless of its name and history, that refuses to acknowledge Jesus Christ as the unique Savior of the world is an instrument of Satan, who has "blinded the minds of the unbelieving so that they might not see the light of the gospel of the glory of Christ, who is the image of God" (2 Corinthians 4:4).

However, the primary focus of *The Divine Defense* is recognizing and defeating Satan's plan against believers. In the next chapter, we will discover how Satan uses his demons to accomplish his purpose for our lives.

WHAT DEMONS WANT TO DO TO YOU

Satan hates you and has a terrible plan for your life

> The demon enters, it is true, as a squatter and
> not as an owner or a guest or one who has a
> right to be there. He comes in as an intruder and as
> an invader and enemy. But come he does if the door
> is opened by serious and protracted sin.
> —MERRILL F. UNGER

The primary focus of *The Divine Defense* is recognizing and defeating Satan's plan against believers. Satan hates you and has a terrible plan for your life. If he cannot succeed in robbing you of eternal life, he will do everything in his power to deprive you of the joy, influence, and rewards that come from serving God in this life. Remember his threefold strategy? He wants to:

- discourage you from worshiping God
- distract you from serving God
- deceive you into disobeying God

How Demons Work

Since Satan cannot be in more than one place at a time, he has delegated much of his work to demons who discourage, distract, and deceive through a variety of means.

Through Nature

Since Satan is referred to as "the ruler of this world" (John 12:31) and "the prince of the power of the air" (Ephesians 2:2), it is reasonable to assume that he and his demons have some control over the elements of nature such as wind, rain, hurricanes, and tornadoes. Living in a city that was almost leveled by a tornado, I can assure you that nothing is more discouraging to Christians than seeing their homes and possessions completely destroyed in an instant. Remember that it was Satan (or one of his "wind demons") who directed a "great wind" to collapse the home of Job's oldest son, resulting in the deaths of all Job's children (Job 1:19).

Through Illness

To blame every illness on demonic activity is neither logical nor biblical. Some of our illnesses are the result of our inhabiting sin-infected bodies. Because our bodies have inherited Adam's curse, we contract illnesses and die. Other times, our diseases are precipitated by poor lifestyle choices: too many trips to McDonald's, too few trips to the gym, or hurtful addictions to things such as alcohol, nicotine, drugs, or Häagen-Dazs vanilla ice cream (now you know mine).

Though not all illnesses are caused by Satan and his demons, some of them are. In describing Jesus's ministry of healing, the gospel writers distinguished between sicknesses that were caused by demons and those that were not.

> When evening came, after the sun had set, they began bringing to Him all who were ill *and* those who were demon-possessed.... And He healed many who were ill with various diseases, *and* cast out many demons. (Mark 1:32, 34)

If every illness had been caused by demons, Mark would have recorded that the people were bringing to Jesus all who were demon-possessed instead of those "who were ill *and* those who were demon-possessed." Obviously,

Mark is telling us there were some people who were physically sick but not under demonic influence.

Through Mental Disorders

Again, it is a mistake to say that all mental illness is directly attributable to demons. When I asked a Christian psychiatrist about the relationship between mental illness and demonic activity, she responded with her own question: "If mental disorders are the result of demonic activity, then why do the symptoms almost always disappear when treated with the right drugs?" Good question.

Our thoughts and emotions are directly traceable to a series of electrical and chemical impulses in the brain. When the brain does not function properly, drug therapy can help restore the natural balances that God intended. However, our thoughts and emotions are more than a series of electrical and chemical impulses. There's an immeasurable, though very real, spiritual component that influences our thoughts and emotions. Positively, this spiritual component can protect us from anxiety and its attendant consequences:

> Be anxious for nothing, but in everything by prayer and supplication
> with thanksgiving let your requests be made known to God. And the
> peace of God, which surpasses all comprehension, will guard your
> hearts and your minds in Christ Jesus. (Philippians 4:6–7)

We will discuss how to apply this passage in a later chapter; my point here is that if a positive spiritual exercise like prayer can influence our thought processes by removing anxiety, then it is reasonable to conclude there are also negative spiritual influences that can seize control of our minds and emotions. While not all mental disorders are caused by external spiritual forces such as demons, some of them are.

Consider the man in Luke 8 who was controlled by numerous demons. A refusal to put on clothes, withdrawal from others, strange voices emanating from his mouth, and deep depression were symptoms that today would immediately land him in a mental hospital. Yet as soon as the demons left him, notice the immediate and radical change in his mental state and behavior:

> The people went out to see what had happened; and they came to Jesus, and found the man from whom the demons had gone out, sitting down at the feet of Jesus, clothed and in his right mind; and they became frightened. Those who had seen it reported to them how the man who was demon-possessed had been made well. (Luke 8:35–36)

The restoration of this man's mental health did not require years of psychotherapy or drug treatment, because his root problem was not primarily physical or emotional, but spiritual. Please understand that I'm not condemning psychotherapy or chemical treatment. Strong biblical counsel and appropriate drug therapy are tools God can use to bring emotional healing to people. What I am suggesting is that sometimes there is also a spiritual component to mental disorders we should not ignore.

Through Suicide

One variety of mental disorder that is almost always attributable to demonic activity is suicidal thoughts. Mark relates the story of a young boy who was possessed by an evil spirit that often threw "him both into the fire and into the water to destroy him" (Mark 9:22). Our natural tendency is to protect our life, not destroy it. An inclination to harm ourselves is unnatural (or better, supernatural).

In John 8:44, Jesus refers to Satan as "a murderer" and "a liar." It's no accident that the Lord associates those two activities with each other. One of the strategies Satan uses in his attempt to rob us of our life, our influence for God, and our future rewards is to persuade us that we would be better off dead than alive.

"Your situation is hopeless." "You've become a burden to others." "No one needs you." These are just some of the lies Satan or his minions whisper to us when we are most vulnerable to discouragement.

You or someone you know can no doubt relate to what I'm writing about. The thought of taking your own life may have come and gone quickly. *I wonder what would happen if I veered into that lane of oncoming traffic,* you might have mused while driving on a busy interstate as your kids screamed at one another in the backseat. We all have those thoughts occasionally, don't we? (Please say yes!) At other times, such ideas are more serious and less easily dismissed from our minds.

May I speak to you as one who has witnessed more times than I care to remember the devastating effects of suicide? The results for the victim of suicide are obvious. But for the family and friends who are left behind, the consequences are unbearable and unending. Having attempted to comfort inconsolable mates who found their spouses blown apart by a shotgun blast or parents who have discovered their teenage child hanging by a rope in a closet, I'm convinced the cruelest and most selfish act anyone can commit is to take his own life. Unless your goal is to inflict as much pain as possible on the people who love you the most, refuse to listen to the lies of the one who hates you the most.

Through Other People

Demons can use other people to discourage, distract, and deceive us. In extreme instances, demons have the ability to use human agents to persecute and murder other Christians. John attributes the slaughter of God's people during the coming Great Tribulation to demonic activity (see Revelation 18:2, 24). We have witnessed similar persecution throughout history and in many areas of the world today.

One of my most vivid memories from a trip to Israel a few years ago is touring the Holocaust History Museum in Jerusalem. To see the photographs and newsreel footage of the horrific atrocities committed against six million Jews in the 1940s was further evidence to me of the reality of demons. Such cruelties against women and children are beyond any reasonable explanation. I believe that the power behind Adolf Hitler and his henchmen originated from the pits of hell, just as it will during the final persecution of the Great Tribulation.

But demons can inspire people to attack us in ways more subtle than torture and murder. If demons are going to deceive us into disobedience, deception will sometimes be wearing a dress or suit. Perhaps you're feeling especially
lonely because of physical or emotional distance from your mate when you
accidentally bump into an old flame from many years ago. A pleasant conversation is followed by an overt invitation from the other person to rekindle that
old feeling. What is it that inspired that person to be at the wrong place and
make such an offer at the wrong time? If indeed Satan and his forces have a
blueprint for your destruction, there are no accidents.

Sometimes demons use other people to discourage us. As spirit beings,
demons lack vocal chords. If they want to communicate with us directly, they
must use the voice of another person just as the demon named Legion spoke
to Jesus through the man he controlled. When someone spews words of discouragement, accusations, lies, and bitterness in our direction, he is allowing
himself to be a mouthpiece for "the accuser of our brethren" (Revelation 12:10)
and his demonic forces.

A person does not have to sprout horns and carry a pitchfork to be a tool
of Satan. Just this past week, one of the leaders in our congregation asked if he
could visit with me after a meeting. For nearly an hour he unloaded every kind
of accusation against me, my leadership, and the church that you can imagine. That night I could not sleep as I replayed his words over and over in my
mind. The next day I was paralyzed by discouragement and fear. *Is he alone in
his beliefs or is he representing a large group in the church?* I wondered.

Even though I was working on this chapter at the time, it took me nearly
twenty-four hours to recognize this assault as being demonically inspired. The
forces of darkness were attempting to discourage me from my work as a pastor and succeeded (at least for a day) in keeping me from exposing those forces
through my writing! No, I'm not suggesting that all criticism comes from
demons. Reproofs that are based on truth and are rooted in a desire to genuinely help someone are gifts from God that should be welcomed, as Solomon
reminds us: "Poverty and shame will come to him who neglects discipline, but
he who regards reproof will be honored" (Proverbs 13:18).

But when a verbal attack, like the one I experienced, is based on lies and bathed in bitterness, its origin is not difficult to determine. Even though the words may come from the mouth of an employer, a friend, a family member, or even a Christian leader, if they are not founded on truth and spoken in love, they may be demonically inspired.

Can Christians Be Demon Possessed?

I imagine the previous section raised a question in your mind. "Robert, are you saying that Christians can be demon possessed?" you may be asking. Although we use the phrase *demon possessed* regularly to refer to people who seem to be under Satan's influence, there is no such phrase found anywhere in the Bible. Never does the Bible refer to someone as being demon possessed. Instead, the New Testament writers used the term *demonized* to describe someone who is under the influence of evil (this is the meaning of the Greek word used in Luke 8:27, to describe the man most English translations describe as being "possessed with demons").

Can a Christian be possessed or owned by Satan and his demons?

Absolutely not.

In Ephesians, Paul declares that believers are "God's own possession," and His identifying mark of ownership on our lives is the Holy Spirit:

> In Him, you also, after listening to the message of truth, the gospel of
> your salvation—having also believed, you were sealed in Him with the
> Holy Spirit of promise, who is given as a pledge of our inheritance,
> with a view to the redemption of God's own possession, to the praise
> of His glory. (Ephesians 1:13–14)

The moment you trust in Christ as your Savior, God permanently marks you as His property by giving you His Spirit. Since God has never been One to believe in joint ownership, if you belong to Him, you cannot be *possessed* by anyone else.

Possession Versus Influence

The real question is not whether Christians can be *possessed* by demons, but whether Christians can be *influenced* by demons. Yes, they absolutely can be demonically influenced. Consider an exchange between Jesus and the apostle Peter. After the Lord revealed to His disciples His impending crucifixion and resurrection, Peter attempted to persuade Jesus that such suffering was unnecessary.

> Peter took Him aside and began to rebuke Him, saying, "God forbid it, Lord! This shall never happen to You." (Matthew 16:22)

Jesus immediately recognized the origin of this temptation to bypass the cross and circumvent God's plan for the redemption of mankind. Peter was simply acting as a mouthpiece for someone else.

> But [Jesus] turned and said to Peter, "Get behind Me, Satan! You are a stumbling block to Me; for you are not setting your mind on God's interests, but man's." (Matthew 16:23)

Jesus was not implying Peter was possessed by Satan, but that he certainly was being influenced by Satan. Some theological types might argue, "Yes, but that happened before the Day of Pentecost when God sent the Holy Spirit to permanently indwell believers. Today Christians cannot be influenced by Satan like Peter was." Really? Consider the experience of two Christians who were controlled by Satan (or his demons) *after* Pentecost.

Ananias and his wife, Sapphira, were members of the church in Jerusalem. As such, there is no reason to suspect they were not genuine believers. However, in an attempt to receive the same kind of adulation that was heaped on another church member named Barnabas (he had sold property and given all the proceeds to the church), this couple also made a generous gift to the church. They lied, however, saying they had given all the money to God's work when, in fact, they kept a portion of the sale price for themselves. The apostle Peter, understanding from personal experience how Satan can influence Christians, confronted Ananias.

> Why has Satan filled your heart to lie to the Holy Spirit and to keep
> back some of the price of the land? (Acts 5:3)

As a result of their sin, both Ananias and Sapphira were struck dead by the Holy Spirit of God before the eyes of the entire congregation! (My friend Howard Hendricks says that this would have been a perfect time for Peter to pass the offering plate and take the largest collection in the history of the church.) Although Ananias was a believer who was indwelt by the Holy Spirit (remember, this event occurred after the coming of the Holy Spirit to every believer at Pentecost), his heart was "filled" (the word means "controlled") by Satan.

How can someone be indwelt by the Holy Spirit and also be filled with Satan at the same time? As I discussed more fully in a previous book, *I Want More!* there is a difference between what the New Testament calls the baptism with the Holy Spirit and the "filling by the Holy Spirit." Every person who trusts in Christ is immediately *baptized* with the Holy Spirit. The baptism with the Holy Spirit is the one-time act of God by which a Christian is joined together with Jesus Christ and is permanently indwelt by the Holy Spirit. The baptism with the Holy Spirit is not some kind of spiritual upgrade that is available only for those who want a first-class experience in their relationship with God. It is part of the basic package for every Christian, as Paul reminded the Christians in Corinth:

> For by one Spirit we were *all* baptized into one body, whether Jews or
> Greeks, whether slaves or free, and we were *all* made to drink of one
> Spirit. (1 Corinthians 12:13)

While every Christian is indwelt by the Holy Spirit, not every believer is empowered by the Holy Spirit. The biblical term for being controlled by God's Spirit is the word *filled.* While Christians are never commanded to be baptized with the Spirit (that's God's responsibility), we are commanded to be filled with the Spirit (that's our responsibility).

> Do not get drunk with wine, for that is dissipation, but be filled with the Spirit. (Ephesians 5:18)

The word translated "filled" is a nautical term that refers to the filling of a ship's sail with wind. The ship is filled or controlled by the wind. Similarly, Christians are to allow themselves to be directed by the Holy Spirit of God. Unlike the baptism with the Spirit, which is a one-time experience, the phrase "filled with the Spirit" denotes a continuous action. We must daily, if not hourly, decide what is going to direct our lives: God's will, our will, or Satan's will.

What does this short treatise on the Holy Spirit have to do with demons? While no Christian can be possessed by a demon, we can be influenced by demons. Any area of our lives that is not controlled by the Holy Spirit is vulnerable to being controlled by Satan and his forces.

You may remember from physics that nature abhors a vacuum. The same truth applies to the spiritual realm. Some spiritual force is going to fill or control your life. Any area of your existence—finances (think Ananias and Sapphira), marriage, work, morality—that is not being directed by the Holy Spirit is vulnerable to being controlled by demonic influences.

I illustrated this truth to our congregation recently with an object lesson. I used a crystal glass to represent my life, and I filled it to the top with clear water representing the Holy Spirit. "Is it possible for me to put anything else in this glass?" I asked. "No!" they shouted back. Then I took another glass and only filled it halfway, asking, "Is there any room remaining for something else to be placed in the glass?" My intellectually astute congregation answered, "Yes!" I then took a can of Diet Coke and poured the dark liquid (representing demonic influence) into the glass. Any area of my life that is not under the Spirit's control is available to be filled or controlled by Satan and his forces. The key to resisting demonic influences in our lives is to make sure that every area of our lives is filled or controlled by God.

Can Christians be possessed by demons? Absolutely not.

Can you and I be influenced by demons? Without a doubt.

How do we prevent areas of our lives from coming under the control of Satan and his forces? And if we realize that some part of our lives has become demonized, how can we reclaim that area from Satan's stranglehold?

In the second part of this book we will discover how to use the six supernatural weapons God has given us as part of the divine defense. But before examining these six strategies, we need to understand the primary way Satan and his demons influence our lives.

Winning the Mind Games

You are what you think

> Good thoughts bear good fruit, bad thoughts
> bear bad fruit—and man is his own gardener.
> —James Allen

In his book *Among the Heroes,* author Jere Longman describes in horrifying detail the extensive preparations made by the terrorists who seized control of United Flight 93 on September 11, 2001, which crashed into a field outside Shanksville, Pennsylvania. The hijackers believed they were involved in a holy war against the forces of evil and prepared accordingly.

> By now, the morning of September 11, the four Islamic men in first class were to have made an oath to die, showered, shaved the excess hair on their bodies and splashed themselves with cologne. They had been given detailed handwritten instructions on how to prepare for their final hours on earth.... The letter was to have been read the previous night. It was a spiritual and practical guide on how the terrorists should fortify against self-doubt and infighting, on how they should prepare to enter paradise by killing their victims and themselves....
>
> They should have blessed their bodies by reading the Koran. By a rubbing of the hands, they should have also blessed their luggage, clothes, knives, IDs, passports, papers.

"Check your weapons before you leave and long before you leave. You must make your knife sharp and must not discomfort your animal during the slaughter."

They should have tightened their clothes before the battle. They should have secured their shoes and worn socks to make sure their feet would stay in their shoes. They should have said a morning prayer in a group....

"Oh Lord, take your anger out on [the enemy] and we ask you to protect us from their evils." And: "Oh, Lord, protect me from them as you wish." And: "Oh Lord, block their vision from in front of them so that they may not see."

When the confrontation began, they were to clench their teeth and "strike like champions who do not want to go back into this world." They were to shout, "Allahu Akbar" (*God is Great*), "because this strikes fear in the hearts of the infidels."[1]

Prayer, mental focus, sharpening knives, the tightening of clothes, and securing shoes and socks were required. These well-trained hijackers knew such preparation was essential for going into battle if they were to have any hope of defeating their adversaries. Now contrast that serious preparation with the lackadaisical approach of most Christians in the battle against our enemy. Even those of us who give intellectual assent to the reality of Satan and who are aware of his intentional plan to destroy us use a hit-or-miss approach.

We find time to read our Bible only if there is nothing interesting on television.

We pray only when we feel our backs are up against the wall.

We possess little knowledge of our opponent or his methods.

We allow the Enemy to distract us, enabling him to deliver a blow when we least expect it.

We refuse to use the supernatural power God has given us.

We believe the Enemy's lie that we are effectually powerless against his attacks.

No wonder so many Christians fall into the trap of immorality, experience the destruction of their marriages, lose in their war against depression, compromise their integrity, and even abandon their faith. With such a passive attitude toward the aggressive assaults Satan has launched against them, these believers are destined to be defeated.

Contrast the passivity of most Christians with the intense and intentional preparation the apostle Paul suggests in our spiritual war against Satan:

> Finally, be strong in the Lord and in the strength of His might. Put on the full armor of God, so that you will be able to stand firm against the schemes of the devil. For our struggle is not against flesh and blood, but against the rulers, against the powers, against the world forces of this darkness, against the spiritual forces of wickedness in the heavenly places. Therefore, take up the full armor of God, so that you will be able to resist in the evil day, and having done everything, to stand firm. (Ephesians 6:10–13)

Be strong.
Put on.
Stand firm.
Take up.

These phrases describe a soldier who is alert and armed for an enemy attack rather than one who is snoring soundly while bombs burst and bullets buzz overhead. The reason you and I must take such a proactive approach against the Enemy is because we are in a "struggle," as Paul describes it, referring originally to a Greek wrestling match.

A few years ago our church invited World Wrestling Entertainment champion Ted DiBiase, the Million Dollar Man, to share his testimony with our congregation. Our staff suggested that before the service we stage an event between DiBiase and yours truly (my performing name was Gorgeous George) in a wrestling ring set up in our parking lot. Several thousand of the curious faithful showed up to witness their pastor, donning a long blond wig, and DiBiase "wrestle" one another. Of course, it was all make-believe. Before the match, Ted and I had carefully choreographed our moves to ensure the contest appeared genuine.

But in Paul's day, wrestling events were actual life-and-death struggles in which the loser of the event would have his eyes gouged out before he was killed. Paul says that is the kind of struggle in which you are engaged with your spiritual adversary, the devil.

Obviously, such a serious threat demands intensive preparation. If you are planning to win your struggle against Satan, you must understand that the primary battlefield on which this war will be waged is your mind.

THE DEVIL AND YOUR MIND

We know from anatomy that the brain is command central for our entire body. Every action, every response, every impulse originates from that vital organ. But the mind is more than a mass of tissue and blood cradled in the cranium. Our thoughts have a spiritual component to them as well. It is a tremendous mistake to attempt to separate the spiritual from the psychological and physical components of life. God created us as body, soul (our mind, will, and emotions), and spirit (our God-consciousness). There is no conflict in our lives that is strictly a spiritual issue, because there is never a time when the spirit is divorced from the body.

Likewise, there is no turmoil in our lives that is solely psychological or physical, because our spirit, along with God's Spirit within us and demonic spirits around us, is always present as well. Someone very clever said that the body, soul, and spirit are so closely connected that if one catches a cold, the other two sneeze!

The writers of Scripture understood that every action, every emotion, and every decision originates in the mind. The writer of Proverbs observed, "For as [a man] thinketh in his heart, so is he" (Proverbs 23:7, KJV). The Hebrews used the word *heart* to refer to the mind. Consider the most monumental events of your life and how they are related to your mind. Most of the mile-stone events in your life began with a thought:

Your marriage: "I *think* I love this person—I *think* that's how I'm feel-ing—and I will ask her to marry me."

Your education: "After considering different schools, I *think* this one would best suit my career goals and budget."

Your salvation: "I *believe* that Jesus Christ is my Savior, and I am trusting in Him for eternal life."

Your vocation: "After considering my gifts and desires, I *think* I would enjoy working as a…"

Beyond these major decisions, we also face numerous day-to-day choices that enter our lives through the gateway of our minds.

Will I exercise today?

Will I purchase this item I really don't need but want?

Will I watch this TV program?

Will I give this person a piece of my mind?

Our lives are largely the sum total of the large and seemingly small choices we make every day. Whom you marry, where you attend school, what voca-tion you choose, whether or not you decide to watch your diet, the books you read (or don't read)—these all determine the course of your life. If your thoughts are crucial in shaping your destiny, is it any surprise that Satan's pri-mary strategy for controlling your life is by infiltrating your mind? No won-der our minds feel like a battlefield as opposing thoughts and emotions war against one another. Henri Nouwen described the mind as "a banana tree filled with monkeys jumping up and down. It is rarely still or quiet. All these thoughts, like so many chimps, clamor for attention."[2]

Right now I imagine your mind feels like that banana tree Nouwen described. Stop and listen for a moment to the different thoughts screaming for your attention.

You don't have time to be reading this book.

Wouldn't it be fun to…

I wonder if…is upset with me.

If only I had…

I'm not implying that every thought is good or evil, godly or satanic. My impulse to stop typing this chapter and go get a hamburger for lunch, my decision to wear a blue tie rather than a red one, or my curiosity concerning a telephone message I was just handed are neither good nor evil, godly nor demonic. What I am suggesting is that when either God or Satan wants to influence us, they will do so through our thoughts. The mind is the primary conduit through which supernatural forces, good or evil, enter our lives. Consider how God's offer of supernatural peace comes through your mind:

> Finally, brethren, whatever is true, whatever is honorable, whatever is
> right, whatever is pure, whatever is lovely, whatever is of good repute, if
> there is any excellence and if anything worthy of praise, [let your *mind*]
> dwell on these things.…And the God of peace will be with you.
> (Philippians 4:8–9)

As we will see in the part 2, anxiety is a paralyzing emotion that originates in the mind. Thus, it only makes sense that God's antidote to anxiety—centering your thoughts on those things that are pure, lovely, and true—would also be introduced through the mind. If your mind (so closely connected to your spirit that they are practically indistinguishable from each another) is the channel through which God communicates, we should not be surprised that it is also the medium through which Satan attempts his greatest influence. Hannah Whitall Smith makes an important observation:

> There are voices of evil and deceiving spirits, who lie in wait to entrap
> every traveler entering these higher regions of spiritual life. In the same
> epistle that tells us that we are seated in the heavenly places in Christ,
> we are also told that we shall have to fight with spiritual enemies. These
> spiritual enemies, whoever or whatever they may be, must necessarily
> communicate with us by means of our spiritual faculties, and their

voices, as the voice of God, are an inward impression made upon our spirit. Therefore, just as the Holy Spirit may tell us by impressions what the will of God is concerning us, so also will these spiritual enemies tell us by impression what is their will concerning us, though not, of course giving it their name.[3]

Satan's Four Channels of Communication

How, precisely, do Satan and his demonic forces attempt to seize our thoughts and consequently control our actions and destiny?

Through Natural Desires

The Apple computer I am using to type these words came with an installed operating system that governs its functions. No engineer in Silicone Valley has to directly communicate with it in order to control its operations. What it will do, and not do, has already been loaded into the computer itself.

Similarly, you and I are each born with an operating system that influences our everyday choices. Unfortunately this operating system is highly defective. It is programmed to instinctively resist God's desires for our lives. When God says, "You shall," it automatically responds, "I shall not." When God says, "You shall not," its initial response is "I shall." This flawed operating system—called the flesh in Scripture—is the result of Adam's initial decision to rebel against God's prohibition in the garden (Romans 5:12). As we saw in chapter 2, Adam and Eve's decision was largely influenced by Satan's initial rebellion in heaven.

Thus, in a real sense, at birth we come out of the box with Satan's rebellious spirit against the Creator already present in a natural bias against God. Even if Satan were destroyed tomorrow, the world would still be filled with murders, immorality, greed, and idolatry. That is why James omits Satan entirely from the sin formula we looked at in the previous chapter: "But each one is tempted when he is carried away and enticed *by his own lust*" (James

1:14). Although James believed in the reality of Satan ("Resist the devil and he will flee from you," James later advised in 4:7), he recognized that the devil's primary influence in our lives is through our corrupt desires.

Nevertheless, Satan cannot rely solely on our defective nature to do his dirty work. He understands—sometimes more than we do—that at the time of our salvation a much more powerful operating system was installed within us (the Holy Spirit). That is why Satan and his minions must resort to other channels of communication.

Through Other Methods

When Satan approached Eve in the Garden of Eden, she did not yet possess a fallen nature, so he had to communicate with her directly. However, if Satan had appeared to Eve in his true monstrous form (Revelation 12 pictures him as a great red dragon with seven heads and ten horns), I doubt she would have hung around for an extended conversation. She would have run as quickly as her feet could have carried her back into Adam's arms.

Instead, Satan chose to make his appeal to Eve by inhabiting the most beautiful creature in the garden, the serpent. Prior to Adam and Eve's rebellion against God, the serpent was not the scaly, scary reptile we think of today. He walked uprightly (see Genesis 3:14) and apparently was of such beauty that he captivated Eve's attention. Is there a better method through which Satan could voice his temptation?

How about this one? Imagine a talking box in your home that sparkles with colorful, alluring images, seducing you with enticing offers: sex without commitment, wealth without work, disobedience without consequences (just to name a few)? So enchanting is this talking box that the average American cannot turn it off. The invitations to evil pour into every home for an average of 8 hours a day, 365 days a year. I'm sure you get the idea; Satan has the ability to use a neutral method, whether a beautiful serpent or a television set, to communicate.

Beyond television, movies, Internet sites, magazines, and books, demonic forces use other neutral means to communicate with us. Horoscopes, Ouija boards, divination, and other channels for supernatural communication are all prohibited in Scripture—not because these methods possess power of their own—but because Satan can manipulate them to influence our decisions.

Through Other People

We have already seen that Satan and his demons often speak to us through other humans. In the case of the demon-controlled man who lived among the tombs, demonic forces used the voice of an unbeliever to communicate with Jesus.

In the case of the apostle Peter with Ananias and Sapphira, Satan communicated through the voice of believers. Realizing that Satan and his demons do have the capability of speaking to us through other people should cause us to carefully evaluate every word spoken to us whether it comes from an employer, a friend, a family member, or even a Christian leader.

How can we discern if the words spoken are actually Satan's words? When you are in doubt, consider the following three questions:

- **Are these words true?** Remember, Satan is the "father of lies" (John 8:44). When someone attacks you with railing accusations that have no basis in fact, he is simply allowing himself to be a mouthpiece for the one labeled by the Bible as "the accuser of our brethren" (Revelation 12:10).

- **Do these words motivate me to trust more or to fear more?** Satan loves to plant doubts in your mind that paralyze and immobilize you. When someone causes you to question God's goodness, His power over your circumstances, His care for you, or your value to Him, that person is simply doing Satan's work for him.

- **Do these words contradict God's Word?** God had warned Adam and Eve, "In the day that you eat from [the tree of the knowledge of good and evil] you will surely die" (Genesis 2:17). But blatantly contradicting God, Satan said to Eve, "You surely will *not* die!" (Genesis 3:4). Amazingly, Eve chose to take Satan's word over God's word. Unfortunately we often make the same choice to our own detriment.

The Bible is the ultimate filter through which we should evaluate every word we hear, regardless of whose lips say it. The pastor who causes you to question the truthfulness of the Bible, the employer who suggests you not follow the law so closely, the mate who encourages you to place your allegiance to him above your allegiance to God, the temptress who promises no one will get hurt are all communicating, *I know better than God what is best for your life.* Do you really believe them?

Through Direct Means

Sometimes Satan and his forces speak to us without the use of any intermediary. Have you ever had random thoughts pop into your mind and wondered, *Where in the world did that come from?* The thought might be one of overt evil, overpowering fear, or even blatant blasphemy against God. You were probably shocked that you could think such a thought. Yes, some of those thoughts arise out of our corrupt natures, as we discussed earlier. But other times, those ideas are coming straight from the lips of Satan or one of his demons.

Consider the experience of King David, a man God described as "a man after [God's] own heart" (1 Samuel 13:14). Yet, David's close walk with God did not exempt him from hearing occasionally from Satan:

> Then Satan stood up against Israel and *moved David* to number Israel. So David said to Joab and to the princes of the people, "Go, number Israel from Beersheba even to Dan, and bring me word that I may know their number." Joab said,…"Why does my lord seek this thing? Why should he be a cause of guilt to Israel?" (1 Chronicles 21:1–3)

This story illustrates Satan's ability to communicate directly with those of us who are God's children in order to tempt us with evil, crush us with fear, or cause us to question God's character. The problem with conducting this census was that it demonstrated David's reliance on the number of soldiers rather than the power of God for protection. Interestingly, in the parallel account of this event (see 2 Samuel 24:1–2), we are told that it was God's anger against Israel that incited David to conduct the census that would bring God's judgment on the nation.

Contrary to the claims of some, these differing accounts are not contradictory. For some unstated reason, God was angry with Israel and desired to discipline the nation. Although He did not directly tempt David to commit the sin of numbering his warriors, He permitted Satan to tempt David, something the devil was more than willing to do! Thus, God's punishment against Israel for some unspecified sin was His allowing Satan to tempt David.

How can I recognize the voice of Satan channeling through my thoughts? By asking the same questions we discussed in the previous section:

- Are these thoughts true?
- Do these thoughts motivate me to trust more or fear more?
- Do these thoughts contradict God's Word?

Precisely what ideas do Satan and his demons attempt to plant in your mind? The list is endless, yet there are some lies that seem to be his favorites because of their resulting consequences. In the next chapter we're going to expose the most effective lies Satan uses to discourage, distract, and deceive Christians.

SATAN'S FAVORITE MIND GAMES

Four lies that will pull you away from God

> Nurture great thoughts, for you will never
> go higher than your thoughts.
> —BENJAMIN DISRAELI

Is there such a thing as an idle thought? John Ortberg doesn't think so. "Each thought we have carries with it a little spiritual power, a tug toward or away from God. No thought is purely neutral.... Every thought is—at least to a small extent—God-breathed or God-avoidant; leading to death or leading toward life," Ortberg writes.[1]

In the previous chapter we saw that Satan and his demons are capable of communicating with us directly through our thoughts. In this chapter we are going to examine four of Satan's favorite "God-avoidant" ideas that will always pull us away from our Creator. The more we are aware of these lies, the more we will be able to take the offensive in the spirit wars.

FAVORITE MIND GAME NO. 1: DISCONTENT

"You don't have what you need to be happy."
Famed basketball superstar David Robinson once spoke about watching super-superstar Michael Jordan clutch the Chicago Bulls' first championship trophy.

"Here I am," Robinson said, "with five cars, two houses, and more money than I ever thought I'd have. What more could I ask for?... Here's Michael Jordan; he has more than me, and, boy, I'd like to have some of the things he has. But is the world setting a trap for us? What I had should have been plenty. But no matter how much I had, it didn't seem like enough because material things can't satisfy your deepest needs."[2]

It's not the world that's setting a trap for us, but the god of this world who is constantly baiting us with the lie that only the things we don't *yet* possess will satisfy our deepest yearnings. Satan used the same line with Eve. Although God had provided the first couple with an idyllic garden setting filled with thousands of trees to enjoy, Satan zeroed in on the one tree from which God had prohibited them to eat and said, "That fruit is what you really need. Eat it and you will experience joy beyond your wildest imagination."

Today Satan continues enticing you and me with the same deception. "If only you had *that* mate, *that* house, *that* job, *that* amount of money, *that* vacation, that car, *then* you could be truly happy. But, alas, God has kept those things out of your grasp and is cheating you out of the happiness you deserve."

What happens when we fall for that deception? James describes the fallout of discontent, beginning with the most obvious consequences of dissatisfaction and then tracing those consequences to their ultimate source.

> For where jealousy and selfish ambition exist, there is disorder and
> every evil thing.... What is the source of quarrels and conflicts among
> you? Is not the source your pleasures that wage war in your members?
> You lust and do not have; so you commit murder. You are envious and
> cannot obtain; so you fight and quarrel.... You adulteresses, do you
> not know that friendship with the world is hostility toward God?
> Therefore whoever wishes to be a friend of the world makes himself
> an enemy of God.... Resist the devil and he will flee from you. (James
> 3:16; 4:1–2, 4, 7)

To understand what James is saying, let's start with the end of the passage and work our way back to the beginning. Allow me to paraphrase James's words:

> Resist the devil because he is promoting a worldly value system that
> equates money with success, sex with love, and power with purpose.
> When you adopt these values, you will start lusting for those things that
> are outside God's will for your life. That constant craving not only leads
> to turmoil within your life when you disobey God, but it causes dissen-
> sion with others as you jealously crave their possessions and positions.

Don't you see that chain reaction occurring every day? What is it that motivates

- a husband to abandon his mate and children for another woman?
- an employee to inflate his résumé in order to get a leg up on other candidates for a position?
- a businessman to risk imprisonment with an illegal scheme?
- a grown child to alienate himself from his parents because they gave a larger gift to his sibling?

At the root of the chaos and disorder these actions produce is discontent. "To be *really* happy I need a different mate, a better job, or more money."

Favorite Mind Game No. 2: Pride

"You are in control of your destiny"

If, indeed, God cannot be depended on to give us what we need to be happy, then we must start looking out for number one. At the core of pride is the con-viction that I must take care of myself and that I *can* take care of myself.

The connection between discontent, pride, and independence is illustrated in Lucifer's fall from heaven. No longer satisfied with being God's second banana, Satan convinced himself that he needed to occupy the number-one chair in the heavenly boardroom. *"God is too power hungry to ever allow me to be in charge, so I will have to take matters in to my own hands,"* Satan most likely responded.

Stop and think for a moment. What caused Lucifer to think he was capable of running the universe? Why did Lucifer think he could ever be successful in his all-out assault on God's throne? One word: *pride*.

> Your heart was lifted up because of your beauty;
> You corrupted your wisdom by reason of your splendor. (Ezekiel 28:17)

Here's my paraphrase of that passage: "You became intoxicated with your God-given beauty and allowed your thinking to be messed up by your God-given gifts." Psychologists have a term for such warped thinking: *delusional*. Forgetting that he was a creature, not the Creator, Lucifer began to believe that he was responsible for his possessions and position. If he could make it this far on his own, what was to keep him from going all the way to the top? He didn't need anyone else—including God.

It's no surprise that Lucifer used the same flawed logic with Eve. After planting seeds of discontent over the one forbidden piece of fruit that would surely fill her life with joy, Satan then encouraged her to act independently, outside of God's parameters for her life. "Seize this golden opportunity now," the Adversary urgently encouraged. "You may never have a chance like this again."

Forgetting that the beautiful garden, the perfect body, and the hunk of a husband she enjoyed were all gifts from God, she allowed herself to be deluded into thinking she was responsible for her current and future well-being. Forgetting that she too was a creature who only existed because God had filled her nostrils with the breath of life, she brazenly violated her Creator's command.

That same spirit of independence that says we can—and we must—seize control of our lives permeates our society. How many graduation ceremonies have you attended during which the following words from "Invictus" were quoted?

Out of the night that covers me,
Black as the Pit from pole to pole,
I thank whatever gods may be
For my unconquerable soul....
It matters not how strait the gate,
How charged with punishments the scroll,
I am the master of my fate:
I am the captain of my soul.[3]

"No. No. A thousand times no!" says the Lord who created us. We are not the masters of our fates, nor are we the captains of our souls. Instead, the psalmist encourages us to remember:

The LORD Himself is God;
It is He who has made us, and not we ourselves;
We are His people and the sheep of His pasture. (Psalm 100:3)

Although we all make day-to-day choices that appear to determine our futures, those decisions still fall within the boundaries of God's ultimate purpose for our lives. Passengers aboard an ocean liner have numerous choices about when to eat, what activities to participate in, and what clothes to wear. Nevertheless, their final destination is under the control of their captain—and so is ours.

FAVORITE MIND GAME NO. 3: FEAR

"You're all alone"

The great irony of pride and independence is that they do not result in confidence, but in fear and despair. In spite of our self-affirming credos, we eventually learn the hard way that we are not the masters of our fates.

A disloyal mate, a maverick cancer cell, or a random accident each has a way of sobering us to the reality of our helplessness. Having dismissed the notion of believing in a Being greater than ourselves who is controlling our destiny—or at least choosing to leave the security of His pasture and go it alone—we eventually come to believe we *are* all alone in this gigantic universe. We are no more than victims of the capricious acts that nature, Satan, or other people may choose to inflict upon us.

The feelings of aloneness produced by alienation from our Creator eventually result in fear. Adam and Eve, having chosen to take control of their own lives and act independently of God, were immediately overwhelmed by anxiety. It's no accident that the first negative emotion recorded in the Bible is not hatred, jealousy, or depression (those would come later), but *fear*. When God confronted Adam about his disobedience, Adam responded, "I was *afraid* because I was naked; so I hid myself" (Genesis 3:10).

Ironically, the by-product of acting independently from God is not indomitable confidence, but continual apprehension. By freeing ourselves from the notion of a Creator who controls all things, humanity has become enslaved to worry.

In the article "Let's Stop Scaring Ourselves," author Michael Crichton catalogs some of the wild fears that have seized our culture in the last sixty years:

> In 1975 *Newsweek* magazine warned that global temperatures were falling and could result in world-wide famine.
>
> Ten years later, scientists were warning of a rise in global temperatures that threatened the survival of our planet.
>
> In the 1960s we were warned of the dangers of overpopulation, with one global think tank predicting that by 2030 the world population would be 14 billion people.
>
> By the end of the twentieth century, fertility rates had fallen to half of what they were in the 1950s.
>
> We were warned that power lines cause cancer. After $25 billion was spent in relocating power lines or the people living near them, it was discovered that not only are power lines not harmful, but the mag-

netic fields that were feared to be carcinogenic can actually be helpful in some medical treatments.[4]

Killer bees, cancer-inducing deodorants, swine-flu epidemics, economic collapses, giant asteroids, and the anticipated meltdown from Y2K are just some of the other manufactured fears that have plagued society in the last sixty years. The relationship between a society's independence from God and its susceptibility to fear is no coincidence. The more we teach people there is no Supreme Being in control of things, from the orbits of the planets to the minute details of our lives, the more susceptible we become to fear. We obsessively calculate all the things that *could* go wrong.

Satan understands all too well the vicious cycle of fear and independence. Independence from God produces fear, and fear motivates us to act more independently of God as we try to control our own destinies.

Favorite Mind Game No. 4: Bitterness

"You've been mistreated"

I once read a news account of a robber who attempted to steal money from a vending machine. In his effort to break the machine open, he accidentally pulled it over on himself. The thief promptly filed a lawsuit against the convenience store in which the machine was located for the injuries he sustained while robbing the store!

Satan is a lot like that thief. Unwilling to accept responsibility for his pride, which led to his banishment from heaven, Satan had to blame someone for his demotion. God was the biggest and easiest target for Satan's anger. Blinded by bitterness, the devil launched a full-scale assault on God and His kingdom in an attempt to exact revenge for his imagined mistreatment. Every struggle you and I face today can be traced to that cosmic conflict rooted in resentment.

Is it any surprise, then, that one of Satan's favorite mind games is to convince us that we too have been unfairly treated by God or by other people?

After Satan enticed the first couple to sin, God came to Adam and Eve and demanded an explanation for their disobedience. What was their response? Adam pointed his finger at Eve and said to God, "This woman *You* gave me, she made me do it!" (Genesis 3:12, paraphrased).

Eve quickly learned how to play the blame game. When God looked to her for an explanation, she pointed to the serpent. "This slime-ball creature, which, by the way, *You* placed here in the garden, deceived me" (Genesis 3:13, paraphrased).

Do you blame God or anyone else for the unfortunate things in your life? These may include

- your divorce
- your termination from employment
- your financial struggles
- your deteriorating health
- your lack of close friendships

Blaming is certainly more palatable than accepting personal responsibility for your situation. But it also prevents you from receiving the forgiveness you may need and changing the behavior that may have led to your predicament. Satan understands that reality. Part of his game plan for your destruction is to blind you to your need for God's forgiveness and to hold you hostage to the patterns of disobedience that produce so much of the misery in your life. Bitterness is one of the Enemy's most effective blindfolds.

Obviously, there are times when we have genuinely been wronged by other people. Although we cannot control the offenses that others bring into our lives, we can control our responses to those wrongs. We can hold on to bitter wrongs until they metastasize into a cancer of bitterness, destroying us and those around us. Or we can choose to let go of the hurts and move on with our lives (the word *forgive* means "to release"). Holding on to offenses leads to slavery. Releasing offenses leads to freedom.

I remember reading once about the way Africans trap monkeys. They place peanuts in a hollowed-out coconut that has been tied to a tree. The monkey reaches in, takes hold of the nuts, but then is unable to remove its fist. The more the monkey tightens its grip on the peanuts, the more impossible it becomes to extract its hand from the coconut shell. If the monkey simply released the peanuts, it could easily free itself; letting go is essential for experiencing freedom.

One of Satan's favorite traps for us is resentment. Spiritually, we have the ability and the motivation to forgive others because of the forgiveness Christ has offered us. Practically, it only makes sense to release our offenders and move on with our lives rather than be held captive by them. When we are wronged, Satan encourages us to grab hold of the hurt or mistreatment, refuse to let the offender go, demand justice, and demand that he pay for what he did. The tighter we hold on, the more enslaved we become.

Beyond these four lies, there are an endless number of other deceptions that Satan can plant in our mind. But the crucial question is, "How can I win over these mind games Satan plays with me?" We will discover the answer to that question in the next chapter.

PART TWO

STRATEGIES FOR SUCCESS IN THE DIVINE DEFENSE

When Satan Comes Knocking

Strategy 1: Recognize and replace destructive thoughts

> Of all the things we do, we have more
> freedom with respect to what we will
> think of, where we will place our mind,
> than anything else.
>
> —DALLAS WILLARD

When Paul penned his strong words about spiritual warfare to the Christians at Ephesus (Ephesians 6:10–13), he was under arrest in Rome. As Paul observed the Roman guard who was watching him, he must have thought, *The same armor this guard wears to protect himself against the enemy is available to every Christian.* Using the imagery of a Roman soldier's armor, Paul describes the essential pieces of equipment we must put on and use if we are to have any hope of winning our death struggle with Satan.

> Take up the full armor of God, so that you will be able to
> resist in the evil day, and having done everything, to stand firm.
> Stand firm therefore, having girded your loins with truth. (Ephe-
> sians 6:13–14)

THE BELT OF TRUTH

The first piece of equipment Paul describes in this passage is the "belt of truth," as it is called in the New International Version. We tend to think of a belt as a secondary accessory, but in Paul's culture, it was a vital piece of clothing, especially for a soldier. The Roman combatant wore a free-flowing garment called a tunic. However, as comfortable as a loose tunic might be in daily life, it could be lethal in combat. An opponent could grab a portion of the loose tunic and gain an advantage in hand-to-hand combat. Or the solider himself might accidentally trip over his own garment. That's why, before entering into battle, every good solider would tuck his tunic into his leather belt to secure it.

Similarly, Paul is encouraging us to secure any loose thoughts that might trip us up or allow the Enemy to gain an unfair advantage over us in our spiritual struggle. Your mind is the devil's playground. More precisely, your mind is the battleground where the invisible battle for your soul is being waged. It is the primary conduit through which Satan channels his temptations and through which God channels His power. Wrong thoughts lead to wrong choices that invariably trip us up, giving the Enemy an unfair advantage.

We have already identified four favorite mind games, or lies, that Satan uses to lure us into disobedience:

"You don't have what you need to be happy" (discontent).

"You're in control of your destiny" (pride).

"You are all alone" (fear).

"You've been mistreated" (bitterness).

Now, we're going to discover four practical actions you can take to confront these loose thoughts by securing them with the belt of truth.

Action 1: Refuse to feel guilty for wrong thoughts

Imagine you are awakened at 3:00 a.m. by someone pounding loudly on your front door. More than likely, before you open the door, you'll look through the peephole to see who is causing the commotion. If it were a neighbor, a friend, or a family member, you would probably open the door and invite him in. However, if it were a stranger wearing a ski mask and carrying a pistol, you would hopefully refuse entry to the potential intruder.

If you were certain the person seeking entry into your home intended to harm you, would you feel guilty over his wanting to assault you? As he banged on your door, would you lament to yourself, *What is wrong with me that would cause this person to want to hurt me?* or *Why would he choose to rob me instead of my neighbor next door?* No, you would call the police immediately to apprehend the would-be assailant as quickly as possible.

We are not always responsible for the harmful thoughts that come knocking on the doors of our minds, seeking entrance into our lives. Although allowing outside stimuli such as certain TV programs, reading material, or Internet sites to fill our minds can incite thoughts of immorality or greed, we are not always to blame for the *first* assault of these ideas. If you were stranded on a deserted island where there were no computers, TVs, or newsstands, you would still battle against wrong thoughts.

How do I know that? Consider Jesus's experience in the wilderness immediately following His baptism. For forty days Christ was completely isolated. No other people, no newspapers, no e-mail. Yet during those forty days, Jesus was tempted with thoughts of discontent, greed, and pride.

"Since God hasn't provided you with what you need to survive, turn these stones into bread."

"You don't need to wait to reign over the kingdoms of the world; they can be yours now if you are willing to worship me."

"You don't need to follow God's timetable. Demonstrate you are the Messiah now! Put on a spiritual circus to demonstrate you are the Son of God."

Where did these thoughts originate? "The devil *said* to Him" (Luke 4:3)—nowhere in the biblical account of Jesus's temptation does Luke record that the devil appeared to Jesus. Possibly, Satan spoke to the Lord the same way he often communicates with us: through the mind.

Yet did these ungodly thoughts make Jesus a sinner? Of course not! He remained the perfect Lamb of God whose blamelessness qualified Him to be our Savior. If you and I are going to win the mind games, we need to first stop feeling guilty when evil thoughts invade our lives and, instead, learn how to deal with those unwelcome intrusions.

Action 2: Refuse to allow wrong thoughts to linger

If we entertain and embellish wrong thoughts for any period of time, those ideas have a way of transforming into obsessions. These, in turn, result in overt actions or attitudes of disobedience. Pastor and author Charles Stanley vividly demonstrates how toeholds can become footholds, and eventually strongholds, for the devil:

> The initial thoughts the devil sends to us may be just a toehold the first time we entertain those thoughts and dwell on them or fantasize about them. The longer we entertain the thoughts, however, the more likely we are to start making mental plans about how we might act on them.
>
> It is then the toehold of an idea becomes a *foothold*. The more we develop plans for acting on a sinful idea or temptation, the more we find that the foothold has become a *stronghold*. We come to the place where we feel compelled to try out the idea in our behavior. We have fantasized and imagined what it was like to do something, experience something, or try something for so long that we come to the place where we want to act on that idea more than we want to banish the idea.[1]

Go back and slowly read that last sentence. When we reach the point that we are more interested in acting on a sinful thought than we are in dismissing that thought, we are in trouble. How can we prevent our thoughts from turning into strongholds for the devil?

Action 3: Recognize and replace wrong thoughts with God's thoughts

My analogy concerning a burglar attempting entry into your home is flawed in one respect. While we may be successful in preventing an intruder from coming into our home, we cannot keep unwanted thoughts out of our minds. The fact that we are thinking about something means that the alien idea has already gained entry.

Nevertheless, we do not need to allow the intruder to sit down in our favorite chair, engage us in an extended conversation, and announce that since he has been so welcomed, he is taking up residence in our spare bedroom! Instead, we need to follow the apostle Paul's advice for dealing with an undesirable guest:

> We are destroying speculations and every lofty thing raised up against
> the knowledge of God, and we are taking *every thought captive* to the
> obedience of Christ. (2 Corinthians 10:5)

Remembering the words *recognize* and *replace* will help you seize control over wrong thoughts. Use the questions we discussed previously to help *recognize* whether or not a thought could have satanic origin.

Is this thought true?

Does this thought motivate me to fear more or to trust God more?

Does this thought contradict God's Word?

But know that simply labeling a thought as harmful and attempting to dismiss it from your mind is not enough. In fact, the more you try to reject an unwanted thought, the more you will find yourself obsessing over it. Teachers sometimes illustrate the power of suggestion by telling students, "Whatever you do during the next three minutes, do *not* think about pink elephants." Guess what the class will think about for the next three minutes in spite of the teacher's admonition? A herd of pink elephants will stampede through the students' minds!

To dismiss Satan's thoughts we must *replace* them with God's thoughts, just as Jesus did.

When Satan attempted to plant seeds of discontent, Jesus responded by quoting a verse from the Old Testament about God's sufficiency to satisfy our deepest cravings: *"Man shall not live on bread alone"* (Luke 4:4).

When Satan enticed the Lord with thoughts of power and riches, Jesus responded by reciting God's greatest commandment: *"You shall worship the Lord your God and serve Him only"* (Luke 4:8).

When Satan tempted Jesus to act independently from God, the Lord responded once again by quoting the Old Testament admonition: *"You shall not put the Lord your God to the test"* (Luke 4:12).

Jesus understood that the best way to dismiss an unwelcome thought is to replace it with another, more-powerful thought. The best way to dispel darkness is to confront it with light!

When fearful thoughts try to seize control of your life, you can replace those thoughts with the truth that "God hath not given us the spirit of fear; but of power, and of love, and of a sound mind" (2 Timothy 1:7, KJV).

When you are tempted with thoughts of discontent over your financial situation, you can replace those thoughts with the truth that, "We have brought nothing into the world, so we cannot take anything out of it either. If we have food and covering, with these we shall be content" (1 Timothy 6:7–8).

When you are tempted by fantasies of sex with someone other than your mate, you can replace those thoughts with the truth that, "The one who commits adultery with a woman is lacking sense; he who would destroy himself does it" (Proverbs 6:32).

I believe it is this process Paul has in mind when he encourages us to gird our loins with truth (Ephesians 6:14). Our success in spiritual battle depends on confronting any loose thoughts with the truth of God's Word.

Action 4: Remember victory over mind games is possible

Satan continually taunts you with the lies that you are his prisoner, that your mind is under his control, and that you must eventually act upon his suggestions. In reality, Satan has no more control over your life than you choose to allow him to have. Author Neil Anderson illustrates that truth by relating an experience from his childhood:

> When I was a boy on the farm, my dad, my brother, and I would visit our neighbor's farm to share produce and labor. The neighbor had a yappy little dog that scared the socks off me. When it came barking around the corner, my dad and brother stood their ground, but I ran. Guess who the dog chased! I escaped to the top of our pickup truck while the little dog yapped at me from the ground.
>
> Everyone except me could see that the little dog had no power over me except when I gave in. Furthermore, it had no inherent power to throw me up on the pickup; it was my belief that put me up there. Because I chose to believe a lie, I essentially allowed that dog to use my mind, emotions, my will, and my muscles, all of which were motivated by fear. Finally I gathered up my courage, jumped off the pickup, and kicked a small rock at the mutt. Lo and behold, it ran![2]

Satan has no more power over you than that yappy little dog! His authority is based upon the lie that he is still in control of your life. As Anderson suggests, "You don't have to outshout him or outmuscle him to be free of his influence. You just have to outtruth him. Believe, declare, and act upon the truth of God's Word, and you will thwart Satan's strategy."[3] The only way to prevail in the mind games is to recognize and replace destructive thoughts—tighten your loose tunic—by putting on the belt of truth.

Putting Out the Not Welcome Mat

Strategy 2: Do what you know you should do

> The enemy is more easily overcome if he is
> not suffered to enter the door of our hearts,
> but is resisted without the gate at his first knock.
> —Thomas à Kempis

Last year I had the opportunity to visit with Jordan Rubin, author of the best-selling health book *The Maker's Diet,* as we shared a cab together on the way to appear on the same TV program. I thought I might be able to glean some valuable (and free) advice from Jordan as we zoomed along the Atlanta freeway. I asked Jordan what I might do to prevent the colds I caught every winter, which quickly became bronchial infections resulting in the loss of my voice. During the winter months, well-meaning but disease-infected congregants feel the need to communicate both their warm feelings and germs to me via handshakes. It is almost impossible to avoid responding to an outstretched hand, even when it is attached to a watery-eyed, mucus-dripping church member. Even though I try to make a beeline to the nearest bathroom to wash my hands, I'm not always successful.

Jordan listened to my dilemma and then shared a helpful insight. In our world we cannot avoid germs unless we want to isolate ourselves from everyone and everything. However, we can create an environment in our bodies that is inhospitable to germs so that they feel unwelcome and flee to a more-friendly place to set up shop. By changing our dietary, exercise, and hygiene habits, we can prevent many of the illnesses that occur when germs are allowed to establish residence in our bodies.

Jordan's advice is also applicable in protecting our spiritual health. Perhaps you become a little discouraged when you contemplate the subject of spiritual warfare. How could you ever prevent a powerful adversary like Satan from targeting you and your family for destruction? Even if the Adversary left you alone, doesn't the fact that you are "hardwired" to think and act rebelliously against God make spiritual defeat as inevitable as my winter colds?

Although we cannot always prevent the spiritual and emotional attacks that emanate from either our enemy or from our own fallen natures, it is possible for us to create environments in our lives that are inhospitable to those assaults. Rather than allowing those temptations to linger and incubate into full-blown cases of disobedience, we can encourage them to vacate the premises. The more Satan realizes that he has little chance of success with you, the less often he will come knocking on the door of your mind and heart. "Resist the devil and he will flee from you" (James 4:7).

What is the secret to living in a way that makes disobedience to God—and its resulting misery—the exception rather than the rule for our lives? We must learn how to put out the Not Welcome mat at the entrances of our hearts to discourage the Enemy's advances into our lives. The apostle Paul calls it putting on "the breastplate of righteousness" (Ephesians 6:14).

UNDERSTANDING THE BREASTPLATE OF RIGHTEOUSNESS

For the Roman solider, the breastplate was essential for battle. This large piece of metal was molded to cover the soldier's entire torso, protecting vital organs such as the heart, lungs, and bowels from enemy attack.

Remember that, in the Jewish mind-set, the heart did not represent the seat of emotions as it does today. Instead, the heart represented the center of thinking, and the bowels represented the seat of emotions (I wonder what the

Jewish Valentine's Day cards looked like?). Just as the heart and other vital organs need a shield to protect them from physical attack, Paul says we need a covering to protect our minds (the heart) and our emotions (the bowels) from spiritual assaults.

Satan understands all too well the relationship between our minds and our emotions. When I counsel with men who have left their wives for other women, the process I hear from them is always the same:

I *felt* like my wife no longer understood me.

I *felt* like life was passing me by.

I *felt* like I deserved some happiness in life, therefore...

I *decided* to leave.

As we saw in the previous two chapters, wrong thoughts produce wrong actions. Every action is preceded by a decision we make in our minds. But those decisions are strongly influenced by our emotions. Our feelings determine our thoughts, which in turn determine our actions. Thus, an essential key for protecting ourselves from Satan's assaults is to prevent our emotions from being hijacked by the enemy. Paul says the breastplate of righteousness offers that kind of protection.

Before we discover how we "put on" this protective covering, we need to understand what Paul means by "righteousness." The Bible uses the term *righteousness* in three distinct ways.

Self-Righteousness

Sometimes the word *righteousness* is used in a negative sense to refer to our attempts to earn God's approval through our own efforts. The common denominator of the world's hundreds of religions outside of Christianity is the belief that one can merit God's or some god's acceptance through a prescribed set of actions or rituals. God clearly labels such attempts as futile. Through the prophet Isaiah, the Lord declared that "all our righteous deeds are like a filthy garment" (Isaiah 64:6). The phrase "filthy garment" refers to the rags associated with a woman's menstrual cycle. You get the picture.

God is not impressed with the good works of an unbeliever. So, clearly,

Paul was not suggesting that we can protect ourselves from Satan's attacks by this kind of righteousness, which God has described as filthy.

Imputed Righteousness

Other times the Bible uses *righteousness* to refer to imputed righteousness. That simply means righteousness or goodness that has been given to us by God. When you trust in Jesus Christ to be your Savior, God performs an amazing, twofold transaction. First, God takes your sin and imputes it or credits it to Jesus Christ. Jesus voluntarily took responsibility for your sins and paid on the cross the agonizing penalty for them.

But even more astonishingly, God also took all of the righteousness of Jesus Christ and credited it to you. Paul described this incredible twofold transaction this way:

> [God the Father] made Him [Jesus] who knew no sin to be sin on our behalf, so that we might become the righteousness of God in Him. (2 Corinthians 5:21)

Author and pastor Erwin Lutzer offers a helpful illustration of this heavenly transaction. Imagine a book titled *The Life and Times of Jesus Christ.* As you open the book, you discover an account of every good thing Jesus Christ ever did. Alongside that book is another book titled *The Life and Times of [insert your name].* In that book is a detailed description of every wrong action you've ever committed and every evil thought you have ever had. When you trust in Christ as your Savior, God exchanges the covers of those two books. He places the cover of the *Life and Times of Jesus Christ* around your book or life. Thus, when God looked at Jesus on the cross, He saw every sin you ever committed or even thought of committing. God saw all your failures as part of Jesus's life story.

Then God took the cover of Jesus's book and placed it around your life; now when God looks at you He no longer sees your sins, but instead He sees the righteousness of His perfect Son. God views your life story as if it were Jesus's perfect life story. That's what is meant by imputed righteousness.

While imputed righteousness assures us of escaping an eternity in hell, it does not exempt us from the attacks of Satan. If Paul had in mind imputed righteousness when he wrote about the breastplate of righteousness, then he would be saying that our one-time decision to become a Christian is sufficient to protect us against our adversary. But we know that is not the case. Obviously, Paul had another kind of righteousness in mind.

Practiced Righteousness

The type of righteousness that protects us from Satan's attacks is the same kind of righteousness Paul encouraged his pastoral protégé Timothy to pursue:

> But those who want to get rich fall into temptation and a snare and many foolish and harmful desires which plunge men into ruin and destruction....
>
> But flee from these things, you man of God, and *pursue righteousness*, godliness, faith, love, perseverance and gentleness. (1 Timothy 6:9, 11)

The term *righteousness* is a synonym for *goodness* or *obedience*. Unlike self-righteousness, which unbelievers practice to earn salvation, practiced righteousness is a believer's obedience to God's will that is the supernatural result of our salvation or imputed righteousness. Jesus used the imagery of fruit to describe this kind of practiced righteousness:

> Every good tree bears good fruit, but the bad tree bears bad fruit. A good tree cannot produce bad fruit, nor can a bad tree produce good fruit. Every tree that does not bear good fruit is cut down and thrown into the fire. (Matthew 7:17–19)

Imagine one spring day you visit a friend who has an apple tree in his backyard. You notice that the branches are dried up, and there are no apples on it. "I'm afraid your tree is dead," you remark to your friend. "Oh, no, it's not dead!" your friend protests. He runs inside, gathers some apples from the refrigerator, comes back outside, and ties those apples to the dead branches of his tree. "See, my tree is alive!" Tying fruit onto a dead tree doesn't make the tree alive. However, fruit that naturally grows on a tree is the best evidence that the tree is really alive.

The only activity more futile than tying apples to a dead apple tree is trying to attach good works to the life of someone who is spiritually dead to try to make him appear spiritually alive. Practiced righteousness seen in traits such as love, forgiveness, gentleness, self-control, and the other fruit of the Spirit described in the Bible does not transform someone into a Christian but is the by-product of being spiritually alive.

But here is where the apple tree analogy breaks down. An apple tree does not struggle to produce apples. The tree doesn't wake up each morning and say to itself, "I need an extra cup of coffee to get the sap flowing today" or "I think this morning I will sleep in a little later instead of finishing the apple I started yesterday." Apples are the natural product of apple trees that are alive.

But even those of us who have been made spiritually alive through God's grace still have to work at producing spiritual fruit. Let's be honest: it takes a great deal of effort to

- love your mate unconditionally
- hold your tongue when you have a juicy piece of gossip to share
- restrain your anger when you are mistreated
- summon the courage to share your faith with a friend or family member
- maintain a consistent time for Bible study and prayer

Think about this. Birds don't have to be told to practice flying, fish don't have to be admonished to practice swimming, and babies don't have to be urged to practice crying. Apple trees don't have to be encouraged to practice making apples.

But even though God has given Christians both the power and the desire to live obediently, we still face the stiff headwinds of opposition from the remnant of the old nature lingering within us and from the powerful temptations from our adversary. That's why God's Word continually admonishes us to *practice* righteousness:

> Now for this very reason also, applying all diligence, in your faith supply moral excellence, and in your moral excellence, knowledge, and in your knowledge, self-control.… For as long as you *practice* these things, you will never stumble. (2 Peter 1:5–6, 10)

> By this the children of God and the children of the devil are obvious: anyone who does not *practice* righteousness is not of God, nor the one who does not love his brother. (1 John 3:10)

> Let the one who does wrong, still do wrong; and the one who is filthy, still be filthy; and let the one who is righteous, still *practice* righteousness; and the one who is holy, still keep himself holy. (Revelation 22:11)

Simply stated, putting on the breastplate of righteousness is continually exerting the necessary effort to obey God's will in every area of life.

Four Benefits of Obedience

Consistently choosing obedience over disobedience protects us from the Enemy in four specific ways.

Obedience protects us from the consequences of sin

If Satan were a salesman, he would be sued by the Federal Trade Commission for false advertising. He continually makes promises he cannot fulfill and hides the dangerous side effects of the product he's peddling. But for now, like the proverbial snake-oil huckster, Satan is free to keep misleading his customers.

To Eve, the Enemy made the hollow promise that by disobeying God she would become like God. Furthermore, he persuaded Eve to ignore the Warning:

This Fruit Is Hazardous to Your Spiritual Life label. "That warning may apply to others, but not you. You will not die from it," he argued.

Satan continues the same deception today. For example, as a pastor, I regularly see the fallout from infidelity in marriage. When I'm counseling a husband or wife engaged in an extramarital affair, I try to help that spouse visualize the inevitable consequences of the affair…divorce, isolation, shame, financial hardship, possible loss of job, or sexual disease. But the cheating mate usually remains unconvinced. He has fallen under the spell of the Evil One. The ecstasy of drinking from stolen waters has so intoxicated him that he is oblivious to the certain destruction that awaits him.

Solomon, writing from his vast personal experience in this area, vividly describes Satan's seduction into sexual sin as voiced through the lips of the adulteress:

> With her many persuasions she entices him;
> With her flattering lips she seduces him.
> Suddenly he follows her.…
> So he does not know that it will cost him his life. (Proverbs 7:21–23)

In Romans 6, the apostle Paul explains a sobering truth of which most people—including many Christians—are unaware. All of us are slaves to somone. We're either serving God or we're serving Satan. No man can serve two masters, but all of us serve one master or the other.

> Do you not know that when you present yourselves to someone as slaves
> for obedience, you are slaves of the one whom you obey, either of sin
> resulting in death, or of obedience resulting in righteousness? (verse 16)

You are enslaved to whatever—or whoever—controls your life. You can choose to serve God by being a slave to righteousness or you can serve Satan as a slave to lawlessness.

Before we decide which master to serve, it only makes sense to consider the benefits each offers for our service. For example, if you were considering a job from two prospective employers, you would compare and contrast the salary, health coverage, retirement benefits, and working environment each offered. Furthermore, you would want to know something about the character of each employer. Is he compassionate? Can he be counted on to keep his word? Does he have what it takes to succeed?

We are faced with a similar choice in our spiritual lives. We choose whether we want to serve Satan and receive his wages for our service to him or serve God and receive His wages. Before you make that choice, Paul asks you to consider the wages each master offers.

> Therefore what benefit were you then deriving from the things of
> which you are now ashamed? For the outcome of those things is
> death.... The wages of sin is death. (Romans 6:21, 23)

We often use this verse in evangelism to teach that the consequence of failing to trust in Christ as Savior is eternal death or separation from God in hell. While that's certainly true, that is not the primary application Paul has in mind here. He's not addressing unbelievers but Christians who choose disobedience over obedience. The outcome of such a choice is always destruction.

Choosing pride over humility destroys our relationships.

Choosing adultery over fidelity destroys our marriages.

Choosing gluttony over self-control destroys our bodies.

Choosing laziness over diligence destroys our dreams.

Paul was right...the wages Satan offers for disobedience to God is the death of everything we value. That is why it is insane to sin! Thomas Merton vividly described the lunacy of choosing to serve Satan rather than God:

> And to try to be happy by being admired by men, or loved by women,
> or warm with liquor, or full of lust, or getting possessions and treasures:
> that turns you away, soon, from the love of God; then men, women, and
> drink and lust and greed take precedence over God; and they darken His

light…and then we are unhappy and afraid and angry and fierce, and impatient, and cannot pray, and cannot sit still. That is the bitter yoke of sin: and for this we leave the mild and easy yoke of Christ.[1]

Putting on the breastplate of righteousness protects us from the bitter consequences of disobedience.

Obedience protects us from doubt

One of my seminary professors used to say, "Men, nothing will cause more doubt in your life than trafficking in unlived truth." Although his admonition was directed toward those of us who preach and teach God's Word as a vocation, it's applicable to every believer. To continually speak about, sing about, and hear about what a difference Christ makes in one's life—without ever experiencing that difference—will lead to great spiritual confusion and disillusionment.

Today it is fashionable in some Christian circles to deify doubt. Adages such as "It's better to debate a question before settling it than to settle a question before debating it" and "The depth of our doubt is proportional to the depth of our faith" lead some to believe that doubt is natural and even healthy for a Christian.

Certainly doubt can be profitable if it causes us to honestly examine the authenticity of our faith. Doubt can be useful if it motivates us to a further study of God's Word. But doubt—especially regarding our relationship with God—is usually more hurtful than helpful.

Interestingly, doubt is never presented positively in the Bible, primarily because it usually leads to a halfhearted commitment to God which the Bible calls being double-minded:

I hate those who are *double-minded.* (Psalm 119:113)

The one who doubts is like the surf of the sea, driven and tossed by the wind. For that man ought not to expect that he will receive anything from the Lord, being a *double-minded* man, unstable in all his ways. (James 1:6–8)

Cleanse your hands, you sinners; and purify your hearts, you *double-minded.* (James 4:8)

The antidote to doubt is obedience. The more you choose to put on the breastplate of righteousness, the greater assurance you will have that you are indeed a member of God's family. As the apostle John commanded:

Little children, let us not love with word or with tongue, but in deed and truth. We will know by this that we are of the truth, and will assure our heart before Him. (1 John 3:18–19)

Only professions of faith that result in expressions of obedience guarantee that we are truly in possession of eternal life.

Obedience protects us from the loss of heavenly rewards

A. J. Gordon once wrote, "I cannot think of a final divine reckoning which shall assign the same rank in glory, the same degree of joy, to a lazy, indolent and unfruitful Christian as to an ardent, devoted, self-denying Christian."[2] To believe that all Christians—regardless of their degrees, of obedience to God's commands—will experience the same heaven is illogical…and most importantly unbiblical.

Although our self-righteousness before we become Christians has no value to God, our practiced righteousness after we become Christians is of great value to God…and to us. Paul describes a special evaluation that every Christian will experience called the judgment seat of Christ:

For we must all appear before the judgment seat of Christ, so that each one may be recompensed for his deeds in the body, according to what he has done, whether good or bad. (2 Corinthians 5:10)

Since I have written about the subject of rewards in heaven extensively in other works, I will not repeat the material here. But this passage, along with others such as 1 Corinthians 3:10–15, teaches that obedience to God in this life results in eternal benefits in the next life, such as special praise, unique privileges, and exalted positions that disobedient Christians will not experience.

Although our *place* in heaven is dependent on (and assured by) Jesus Christ, our *position* in heaven is determined by our obedience to God's commands. Our entrance into heaven is the result of Christ's work on the cross for us, but our full enjoyment of heaven is the result of our work for Christ here on earth.

Perhaps this illustration will help. Some of you may remember that originally Disneyland was not a one-price amusement park as it is today. Everyone who paid the basic admission price was entitled to a certain number of rides. However, to enjoy certain attractions—especially the E ticket rides like Space Mountain—you had to purchase additional tickets. The first time I went to Disneyland with my brother and sister, my grandfather purchased a book of tickets for each of us that allowed us to enter the park and enjoy a few of the attractions. But if we wanted to do more, we had to pay with our own money.

Everyone who had the basic ticket package was thrilled to be in "the happiest place on earth." But purchasing the additional tickets allowed you to experience a little more happiness than others!

Jesus Christ has paid our admission price into heaven. Everyone who enters through the heavenly gates is assured of an exhilarating time. However, those who are more obedient to God's commands will earn the right to enjoy heaven in a way greater than those who are not obedient.

Whenever I teach on the subject of heaven, there's always someone who says, "I don't care anything about rewards in heaven. Just as long as I make it there, I'll be satisfied."

Yet the Bible teaches that those who enter heaven but fail to receive rewards will experience real, measurable loss:

If any man's work which he has built on [the foundation of Jesus Christ] remains, he will receive a reward. If any man's work is burned up, *he will suffer loss;* but he himself will be saved, yet so as through fire. (1 Corinthians 3:14–15)

Is it really possible that a Christian could experience regret in heaven over rewards he has forfeited through disobedience? Is it conceivable that a disobedient believer would feel the same way I did at Disneyland? *This is a wonderful place, but had I known what experiences awaited me, I would have prepared better to enjoy them.* If Satan can't rob us of our presence in heaven, the next best thing is to cause us to forfeit our rewards in heaven through disobedience.

We need to exercise balance here. As one writer says, "To overdo the sorrow aspect of the judgment seat of Christ is to make heaven into hell. To underdo the sorrow aspect is to make faithfulness inconsequential."[3]

The good news is that there is still time to avoid any regrets in heaven. By putting on the breastplate of practiced righteousness in this life, we protect ourselves against any possible regrets in the next one.

Obedience protects us from Satan's further entrance

Whenever I counsel with Christians who are battling powerful addictions, reaping the consequences of their immorality, or questioning the goodness or even the existence of God, I often think of C. S. Lewis's observation: "The safest road to Hell is the gradual one—the gentle slope, soft underfoot, without sudden turnings,...without signposts."[4]

Satan does not launch a single assault on your heart and mind, storm into your life, and suddenly claim victory. Instead, he is carefully looking for that one compromise that will give him a toehold that will become a foothold and eventually a stronghold in your life. That compromise can be something as seemingly innocuous as allowing a conversation with a member of the opposite sex to cross the line, "borrowing" an item from the office, participating in an Internet chat room just to see what everyone is talking about, or choosing a rerun of *Everybody Loves Raymond* over time in God's Word because you've had a difficult day and need to unwind.

The problem with making one compromise is that it makes the next one easier, and the one after that even easier. As Samuel Johnson said, "The chains of habit are generally too small to be felt until they are too strong to be broken."

Solomon expressed that same truth this way:

His own iniquities will capture the wicked,
And he will be held with the cords of his sin. (Proverbs 5:22)

Imagine taking a piece of string and wrapping it around your hand once. With a simple flick of your wrist you could free your hand. A little piece of string could not possibly overcome the strength of your wrist. But continue to wrap that relatively flimsy piece of string around your hand several times, and you will find it impossible to break free. Similarly, one compromise paves the way for another:

- The first conversation with someone else's mate makes the next one easier.
- The first item taken from your employer makes taking the next one easier.
- The first five minutes spent on an inappropriate Internet site makes the next five minutes easier.
- The first forfeited time alone with God makes forfeiting the next time easier.

Before we know it, we are so enslaved to our wrong choices that we find obedience practically impossible.

Putting on the breastplate of practiced righteousness is the first line of defense against Satan's entrance into our lives. A Haitian pastor illustrated the danger of disobedience—even in seemingly small areas of life—with this parable.

A certain man wanted to sell his home for two thousand dollars. Another man wanted to purchase the home but lacked the necessary financial resources. After a great deal of haggling, the owner agreed to sell the home for half the asking price with one condition: the owner could retain ownership of one small nail protruding behind the front door.

After several years passed, the original owner decided he wanted the house back, but the new buyer was unwilling to sell. So the first owner went out and found the decaying carcass of a dead dog and hung it from the single nail on the front door he still "owned." The stench was so horrible that the house soon became uninhabitable. The new owner was forced to sell the home to the original owner at a ridiculously low price—all because of a single nail.

The Haitian pastor concluded with this application: "If we leave the devil with even one small peg in our lives, he will return to hang his rotten garbage on it, making [our lives] unfit for Christ's habitation."

PUTTING ON THE BREASTPLATE OF RIGHTEOUSNESS

Paul doesn't command us to merely understand the breastplate of righteousness or value the benefits of the breastplate of righteousness but to *put on* the breastplate of righteousness so that we can experience the protection from Satan it affords. How do we do that?

Appreciate the power of habits

I am your constant companion. I am your greatest helper or heaviest burden. I will push you onward or drag you down to failure. I am completely at your command. Half of the things you do you might just as well turn over to me, and I will be able to do them quickly and correctly. I am easily managed—you must merely be firm with me. Show me exactly how you want something done and after a few lessons I will do it for you automatically.

I am the servant of all great people; and alas, of all failures as well. Those who are great, I have made great. Those who are failures, I have made failures. I am not a machine, though I work with all the precision of a machine plus the intelligence of a man. You may run me for profit or run me for ruin—it makes no difference to me. Take me, train me, be firm with me, and I will place the world at your feet. Be easy with me, and I will destroy you. Who am I? I am habit.[5]

In the previous section, we saw how one small act of disobedience can lead to another…and another…and another, until we are held captive by our own compromises. However, habits—repeated patterns of behavior—do not always lead to sin. It's possible to harness the power of habits for our betterment rather than our detriment.

Habits can either work for you or against you. They can be either your servant or your master. But before you can experience the benefits of discipline (another term for good habits), you need to especially appreciate the power of discipline in your relationship to God.

Dallas Willard uses the analogy of a star athlete to illustrate the power of habits. A teenage boy who idolizes a star baseball player may decide that the way to succeed in baseball is to mimic the actions of a star ballplayer during the game; to swing like he swings or slide into first base like he slides. But does mimicking the actions of an athlete in the game lead to greatness?

Of course not.

> The star performer didn't achieve his excellence by trying to behave in a certain way only during the game. Instead, he chose an overall life of preparation of mind and body, pouring all his energies into that total preparation, to provide a foundation in the body's automatic responses and a foundation of strength for his conscious efforts during the game.
>
> Those exquisite responses we see [during the game]…aren't produced and maintained by the short hours of the game itself. They are available to the athlete for those short and all-important hours because of a daily regimen no one sees.[6]

Too often we tell Christians that the secret to obedience in difficult situations is to ask, "What would Jesus do?" and then act accordingly. The only problem is that if we wait until we are in the midst of an attack from the Enemy—or our own corrupt nature—to "do what Jesus did," it's too late to experience success.

Jesus's amazing and automatic obedience in the middle of life crises was the result of His habits of solitude, prayer, meditation on God's Word, and obedience in the smallest details of life. The Christian who expects obedience to come easily when under attack is as doomed to failure as the athlete who ignores the disciplines of diet, exercise, and training yet expects to perform well in the game.

Choose discipline over deliverance

Let's be candid for a moment. Most of us prefer the miraculous to the mundane. It's easy for us to wrap our natural aversion to spiritual disciplines such as Bible study, prayer, financial sacrifice, and obedience in a cloak of spirituality. We seek a one-time fix-it prayer or an ecstatic experience that will forever deliver us from the demons of lust, addictions, or laziness. Yet, as we will see in chapter 12, even if such specific demons do exist, removing them through an act of exorcism does not ensure they will not return.

In a modern version of C. S. Lewis's *The Screwtape Letters*, Randy Alcorn relates a letter from Lord Foulgrin to his demonic student Squaltaint:

> Let them cast us out, or imagine they have, as long as the vermin keep making the daily choices that invite us back in. Let them "name" and "bind" us to their hearts' content as long as they entertain the thoughts and engage in the activities that give us power over them....
>
> It's not power plays and sweeping declarations of our defeat that frighten me, it's the quiet prayers for personal holiness and greater yieldedness to the Enemy [God]. Far better that they focus on us than look to their own hearts and ask the Enemy to cleanse them....
>
> Never frightened by their grandstanding,
> Lord Foulgrin[7]

Cultivating the disciplines of personal prayer, reading God's Word, confession of sin, and consistent obedience threatens Satan's plan for you more than any exorcism or service of deliverance.

Perform an obedience inventory

The great evangelist Charles Finney once observed, "The man who is convicted of one sin is convicted of all. But the man who is convicted of all sins is convicted of none."[8] Putting on the breastplate of righteousness requires more than simply resolving "I will be more obedient to God." Real and lasting change requires repentance (a word that means "a change of mind leading to a change of direction"). But genuine repentance requires specificity.

For example, when the Old Testament priest Ezra confessed his and the Israelites' sins to God, he identified specific ways they had sinned against God and also made specific commitments to remedy their disobedience (see Nehemiah 10:28–39). Ezra understood that the usual "forgive us our many sins and help us to do better" kind of prayer didn't make it past the ceiling of the temple.

I recently read a biography of Benjamin Franklin. Although the great inventor was not a Christian, he strove to improve his character through discipline. Franklin made a habit of selecting one character quality he felt needed improvement and concentrated on it for an entire week. Then, feeling he had mastered that quality of, say, self-control, he would move on to another quality. Obviously, without the power of the Holy Spirit to assist him, Franklin's ability to experience lasting change was limited. But at least he understood the importance of specificity to effect real change.

I encourage you to consider the Life Grid below. Ask God to reveal to you one thing He would like you to stop doing and something He would like you to start doing in each of these life areas.

FAMILY:
I should stop...
I should start...

FINANCES:
I should stop. . .
I should start. . .

SPIRITUAL LIFE:
I should stop…
I should start…

WORK:
I should stop…
I should start…

HEALTH:
I should stop…
I should start…

FRIENDSHIPS:
I should stop…
I should start…

No doubt you're thinking, "But there are so many things I should stop and start in each area. I don't know where to begin." Remember, "the man who is convicted of all sins is convicted of none." The road to effective and lasting change begins with a first step.

Decide that obedience is possible—and profitable

One writer points out that many Christians believe disobedience is as inevitable as the law of gravity. But such thinking is not only erroneous, it is lethal to the goal of obedience.

> Falling off a platform is not a habit. Cultivated lusting, anger, and so on are. And generally speaking, those who say they "cannot help it" either are not well informed about life or have not decided to do without "it."
>
> Most likely, it's the latter. But the really good news here is that the power of habit can be broken. Habits can be changed. And God will

help us to change them—though He will not do it for us—because He has a vital interest in who we become.[9]

Don't fall for one of Satan's most insidious lies: "You *have* to sin." Disobedience is not inevitable. One of the primary benefits of having the Holy Spirit reside in you is the ability to just say no to sin.

> For the power of the life-giving Spirit—and this power is mine through Christ Jesus—has freed me from the vicious circle of sin and death. (Romans 8:2, TLB)

God has provided us with the power to obey. We must provide the willingness to obey.

Have you come to the realization that the long-term consequences of disobedience overshadow any short-term pleasures sin offers?

Do you believe—really believe—that God's plan for your life and eternity are better than Satan's?

Do you desire to protect yourself from the painful consequences of sin, from doubts about your relationship to God, from regrets over the loss of rewards in heaven, and from Satan's further control of your life?

If so, you can put on the breastplate of righteousness right now by doing even one thing you know would please God in each of the above life areas.

God has already supplied you with the desire. All you must supply is the decision.

Putting on Your Soul Soles

Strategy 3: Make God's business your business

> This is true joy in life…being used for a purpose
> recognized by yourself as a mighty one…being a force
> of Nature instead of a feverish selfish little clod of
> ailments and grievances complaining that the
> world will not devote itself to making you happy.
> —George Bernard Shaw

Herb Kelleher, the cofounder of Southwest Airlines, was once asked about the secret of his airline's phenomenal success. "I can teach you the secret to running this airline in thirty seconds," he said. "This is it: Southwest is the low-fare airline. Not *a* low-fare airline. We are *the* low-fare airline. Once you understand that fact, you can make any decision about this company's future as well as I can."

Kelleher elaborated on his statement. "Here's an example. Tracy from marketing comes into your office. She says her surveys indicate that the passengers might enjoy a light entrée on the Houston to Las Vegas flight. All we offer is peanuts, and she thinks a nice chicken Caesar salad would be popular. What do you say?"

The interviewer hesitated, so Kelleher answered his own question. "You say, 'Tracy, will adding that chicken Caesar salad make us *the* low-fare airline from Houston to Las Vegas? Because if it doesn't help us become the unchallenged low-fare airline, we're not serving any d— chicken salad.' "[1]

Understanding your unique purpose is not only integral to success in the business world, it is foundational to success in the spiritual world. A clearly defined life purpose is like a beacon in the dark that provides direction when we face crucial choices.

The slugfest between airlines over passenger share is child's play compared to the spiritual war raging between you and Satan over your destiny. Do you really want to win this war? Would you rather be a victor than a victim? If so, discovering your purpose in life—and then making choices according to that purpose—is essential for victory in the spirit wars.

Shoes Make the Outfit

I once heard a fashion consultant for men say, "I always judge the quality of a man's wardrobe by first looking at his shoes." Good shoes are essential for any well-dressed man or woman. In New Testament times, however, quality footwear was more than just a fashion statement. Sturdy shoes were indispensable in a world where most people walked wherever they traveled. For a Roman soldier in the heat of battle, good boots were critical for his success. The thick soles of the Roman army boot protected the soldier against stones or sharp sticks the enemy might have planted in the ground in order to pierce the soldier's foot.

Pieces of metal protruding from the bottom of the soldier's boots, much like the cleats in athletic shoes today, also provided stability for the soldier, preventing him from stumbling while engaged in hand-to-hand combat with his adversary. As the apostle Paul studied the Roman soldier who guarded him, he noted his thick-soled, metal-enhanced boots and compared them to an essential component for any Christian who wants to win in his death struggle with Satan.

> Stand firm, therefore, having girded your lions with truth, and having
> put on the breastplate of righteousness, and having shod your feet with
> the preparation of the gospel of peace. (Ephesians 6:14–15)

Boots Are Made for Walking

I've discovered the hard way that many respected commentators simply omit this verse in their discussion of spiritual armor because its meaning and application seem unclear. Some who chose to tackle this seemingly difficult verse identify the reference to boots as the assurance of salvation, providing stability under Satan's assaults. But that interpretation seems unlikely, given an-other piece of spiritual armor Paul discusses later: "the helmet of salvation" (verse 17). The helmet is clearly a reference to the assurance of relationship to God.

I believe the key to identifying the boots as an essential piece of our spiritual armor is recognizing that this verse is a paraphrase from Isaiah:

How lovely on the mountains
Are the feet of him who brings good news,
Who announces peace
And brings good news of happiness,
Who announces salvation,
And says to Zion, "Your God reigns!"
      (Isaiah 52:7)

Paul is linking feet with the announcement of Christ's coming salvation anticipated by the prophet Isaiah seven hundred years before Jesus's birth. If you think it's a stretch to interpret Isaiah's words as a reference to announcing Christ's salvation, consider how Paul links Isaiah's words with evangelism (meaning "to announce good news") in his letter to the Christians at Rome:

How will [the unsaved] hear without a preacher? How will they preach unless they are sent? Just as it is written, "How beautiful are the feet of those who bring good news of good things!"...

So faith comes from hearing, and hearing by the word of Christ.
(Romans 10:14–15, 17)

Today the word *preach* is considered a pejorative term, such as when my teenage daughter says, "Dad, quit preaching to me." But in Paul's day the word simply meant "to announce or proclaim." The spread of the gospel message is not limited to paid professionals speaking in a stained-glass voice once a week from a wooden pulpit. Paul is emphasizing the necessity of every believer regularly proclaiming the good news of the salvation offered by Jesus Christ.

Therefore, the spiritual boots that give stability to a Christian's life are his willingness and ability to share the message of Christ with others. Those who challenge this interpretation may ask, "What does evangelism have to do with spiritual warfare? How does our commitment to sharing the gospel with others help us defeat the attacks of Satan?"

These are good questions, for certain. So let's take a moment and discover the relationship between our purpose in life, our evangelism, and our success in spiritual warfare. We'll do this in terms of four simple statements.

You Were Created for a Unique Purpose in Life

Admittedly, not everyone agrees with this first premise. Many non-Christians believe that their existence on planet Earth is simply a biological fluke. The late paleontologist Stephen Gould expressed that view in stark terms:

> We exist because one odd group of fish had a peculiar fin anatomy that could transform into legs for terrestrial creatures; because the earth never froze entirely during an ice age; because of a small tenuous species, arising in Africa a quarter of a million years ago, has managed, so far, to survive by hook and by crook. We may yearn for a "higher answer"—but none exists.[2]

Contrast that bleak assessment of our purpose with God's words to the prophet Jeremiah:

Before I formed you in the womb I knew you,

And before you were born I consecrated you. (Jeremiah 1:5)

God declared to Jeremiah, as He does to all of us, that our existence is no accident. We did not evolve from some primordial chemical broth that oozed over the Earth. Instead, our Creator proclaims throughout the Bible these clear messages:

- I am the One who made you.
- I know everything about you.
- I have set you apart for a special purpose.

Your Purpose Is Connected to God's Purpose

As I pastor, I see many Christians wandering around in a spiritual fog wondering, *Why am I here? What is my purpose in life? What does God want me to do with my life?* I don't want to diminish the importance of discovering God's will for your life (especially since I have written a book on the subject!), but many of your questions about God's plan can be answered by grasping this simple truth: you have been created by God, selected by God, and empowered by God to fulfill His agenda, not yours.

In the first chapter we saw that the New Testament repeatedly compares believers to soldiers in battle. In New Testament times, the primary mission of Roman soldiers was to expand the emperor's kingdom throughout the world. No soldier would wake up in the morning and ask himself, "Why am I here?" "I wonder what I should do with my time today." "What need is there in the world that I can meet?" Those questions had already been answered for the soldier. His job was to serve his commander, not himself. Paul uses that same analogy to remind us of our primary purpose in life:

No soldier in active service entangles himself in the affairs of everyday life, so that he may please the one who enlisted him as a soldier. (2 Timothy 2:4)

You and I have been enlisted (a nice word for *drafted*) to fulfill the mission given to us by our Commander. Just as Jesus came to seek and to save those who are lost (see Luke 19:10), we have been recruited to continue His mission. Simply put, our purpose in life is to join God in *His* purpose of rescuing as many prisoners as possible from Satan's kingdom and turning them into fully committed followers of Jesus Christ. So that no one would misunderstand the mission, Jesus repeated the assignment before He ascended to heaven:

> Go therefore and make disciples of all the nations, baptizing them in
> the name of the Father and the Son and the Holy Spirit, teaching them
> to observe all that I commanded you; and lo, I am with you always,
> even to the end of the age. (Matthew 28:19–20)

Does God need us to fulfill His seek-and-save mission? No, God doesn't need anyone or anything. But God has chosen to allow us to participate in the achievement of His grand redemptive plan for the universe. Partnering with mankind for the achievement of a great purpose has always been God's method of operation.

God created the Garden of Eden but said to the first couple, "You cultivate it and keep it."

In the days preceding the flood, God said to Noah, "I'm going to save you and a few others, but you build an ark."

To Nehemiah, God said, "I am going to change the king's heart so that you may return to Jerusalem, but you build the wall around the city."

To Christians today, God says, "I have sent my Son as the sacrifice for the sins of the world, but you go into all the world and make disciples."

Occasionally, when I am speaking to my congregation about our responsibility to share our faith, expand the outreach of our church, or implement more-effective discipleship ministries, some pseudospiritual saint will say in his most condescending tone, "Now remember, Pastor, it is not up to us, it is up to God to do the work."

Every time I hear that comment I'm reminded of the story of the man who bought a run-down farm. The fields were overgrown with weeds, the fence was falling down, and paint was peeling off the barn. The farmer went to work. He plowed the fields, repaired the fence, and painted the barn. One day the local preacher stopped by to visit. "My, you and God have done a wonderful job with this farm." The farmer, wiping the sweat from his forehead said, "Preacher, you should have seen this place when God had it all to Himself."

No, God doesn't need us to achieve His plan, but He has given us the indescribable privilege of being part of a global enterprise that gives meaning to our existence. Paul David Tripp reminds us how magnificent this is:

> Your life is much bigger than a good job, an understanding spouse, and non-delinquent kids. It is bigger than beautiful gardens, nice vacations, and fashionable clothes. In reality, you are part of something immense, something that began before you were born, and will continue after you die. God is rescuing fallen humanity, transporting them into his kingdom, and progressively shaping them into His likeness—and He wants you to be part of it.[3]

Fulfilling Your Purpose Is the Key to Fulfillment in Life

A city worker once explained his purpose in life: "I dig the ditch to earn the money to buy the food to get the strength to dig the ditch." Sadly, that seems to be the treadmill on which many people find themselves. Get up, go to work, come home, eat supper, sit comatose in front of the tube for a few hours, and go to bed. Even those who are determined to break that cycle and pack their lives with achievement, excitement, fame, or fortune are usually disappointed.

As I wrote these words, the newspapers and airwaves were filled with the accounts of the death of legendary talk-show host Johnny Carson. He reigned over the airwaves for thirty years as the king of late-night television. His fortune was estimated to be in the hundreds of millions of dollars. He lived in a luxurious mansion in Malibu. He traveled the world pursuing his passions for tennis and sailing.

An acquaintance who worked at NBC used to provide me with tickets to *The Tonight Show*. I will never forget the last time I saw Johnny Carson hosting the program. Another king of the entertainment world, Bob Hope, was his special guest on the program that evening. Seated on the front row of the studio audience, I watched those two show-business legends staring blankly during the commercial breaks. They looked as if they would rather be anywhere in the world than where they were, even though many would give anything to be in their places. Whenever I am tempted to fantasize about how happy I'd be if I could only climb one more rung up the success ladder, I think about the miserable expressions on the faces of those two men who had made it to the top.

Many years ago the most successful man of his day lamented about the emptiness of success. King Solomon expressed the inability of work, wealth, or pleasure to fill the vacuum of his life:

> All that my eyes desired I did not refuse them. I did not withhold my
> heart from any pleasure, for my heart was pleased because of all my
> labor and this was my reward for all my labor. Thus I considered all my
> activities which my hands had done and the labor which I had exerted,
> and behold all was vanity and striving after wind and there was no
> profit under the sun. (Ecclesiastes 2:10–11)

Why are we constantly searching for some new pleasure, some new achievement, some new possession, or some new mate to satisfy us, only to be profoundly disappointed?

Here is a simple explanation: eternal beings can only be satisfied by that which is eternal. You can't fill an entire ocean with only one bucket of water. Since, as Solomon observed, God has "set eternity in [our] heart[s]" (Ecclesiastes 3:11), only that which transcends our brief existence on this planet can quench our thirst. We need an eternal companion and an eternal purpose to fill our God-shaped spirit with meaning.

Living My Purpose Helps Me Thwart Satan's Attacks

Adopting Christ's grand purpose is directly related to experiencing success in your spiritual battles against Satan. Living out your purpose means making daily choices, if not hourly choices, concerning every area of your life. The airline executive chooses peanuts over chicken Caesar salad, not because peanuts taste better, but because their low cost helps him achieve his purpose statement for the airline. Similarly, the Christian who makes enlarging God's kingdom his life mission will find it easier to say *no* to Satan by making three critical choices.

Choose purity over immorality

There are a lot of reasons I would not have an affair: I love my wife; I would hate to lose the respect of my children; the emotional and financial costs of a divorce would be overwhelming. But an even more compelling reason to say no to Satan's continual enticements is that a few moments of sexual pleasure would destroy a lifetime of ministry.

Once my disobedience was uncovered (and immorality is almost always discovered), it would disillusion those whom I had led to Christ, as well as those believers who have listened to my teaching of God's Word through the years. Why would I want to wipe out years of work and sacrifice for a few moments of enjoyment?

Keeping your life purpose clearly in mind can be a powerful deterrent to the lure of immorality. For a moment, consider how immorality in your life might thwart your God-given mission:

- How would a member of the small-group Bible study you lead respond if he saw you standing in line for a questionable movie?
- How would the discovery of pornography on your computer at work affect your witness to your supervisor or fellow employees?
- How would the revelation of your illicit relationship with someone affect your children's or your mate's attitude toward God?

Although you may not serve as a paid professional like those of us in vocational ministry, we are part of the same mission: enlarging God's kingdom by encouraging people to become fully committed followers of Christ.

Choose generosity over greed

Immorality is not the only trap the Enemy sets for us. Another powerful temptation you and I wrestle with daily is materialism. We can become preoccupied with money for a variety of reasons. Some of us appreciate the luxuries that money can purchase: an expensive car, designer clothes, a beautiful home. Others enjoy the independence that an accumulation of money affords, the ability to travel whenever and wherever desired, or the freedom to tell an employer to "take this job and——." Still others believe a mound of money can protect them from devastating catastrophes such as unemployment or illness. Regardless of our reason for fixating on money, the result is always the same:

> But those who want to get rich fall into temptation and a snare and
> many foolish and harmful desires which plunge men into ruin and
> destruction. For the love of money is a root of all sorts of evil, and
> some by longing for it have wandered away from the faith and pierced
> themselves with many griefs. (1 Timothy 6:9–10)

A snare is a trap set by a skillful hunter. Satan, a master stalker, understands that money is an effective trap in destroying your relationship with God. A preoccupation with money will always lead us away from God:

- A focus on material possessions destroys our desire for God.
- The independence that money provides us destroys our dependence on God.
- The security money offers us destroys our trust in God.

Jesus bluntly said you can love money or you can love God, but you can't love both (see Matthew 6:24). In the same New Testament passage, He also provides a powerful antidote to a fixation on finances:

Seek first His kingdom and His righteousness, and all these things will be added to you. (Matthew 6:33)

Devoting yourself to a purpose greater than your immediate happiness can drastically alter your attraction to money. Definitively connecting yourself to God's kingdom purpose will dramatically transform your attitude about money.

I've seen such a metamorphosis in a number of our church members recently. As we cast the vision a few years ago for a new twenty-one-million-dollar worship center to help us reach more people in our community with the gospel, I heard a number of stories about financial sacrifices made in order to contribute a significant amount of money. One woman who had planned to retire that year decided to keep working several more years and devote all her income to the project. A couple donated the money they had set aside for an addition to their home. Others refinanced their homes, contributing the equity that had accumulated and extending their mortgage payments many years into the future.

But the common denominator in all the stories was that those who gave sacrificially to this project gained a new interest in what was happening in God's work. One man who contributed a significant amount from his retirement account said, "I used to watch the stock market every day, now I come down to the church and watch the construction project since that is where my money is now invested!"

Mark Twain once gave this bit of investment advice: "Put all your eggs in one basket, and then watch the basket!" The second portion of that maxim is funny but unnecessary. We instinctively focus our attention wherever we have invested our financial resources.

If the bulk of your money is invested in your home, then you will naturally be interested in the housing market.

If the majority of your assets are in the stock market, then it is only natural for you to watch carefully the ups and downs of the Dow Jones Average.

If you decide to play it safe and invest your assets in the bond market, you will naturally watch the rise and fall of interest rates.

"Where your treasure is, there your heart will be also," Jesus observed (Matthew 6:21). The best way to keep your affections centered on God and His kingdom is by investing a significant portion of your assets in the expansion of God's kingdom.

Choose diligence over aimlessness

Purpose is to life what the skeleton is to the body.[4] Understanding clearly why we exist provides a structure that supports and shapes the other components of our lives, including how we spend the most precious commodity God has given us: time. Author John Eldredge makes a confession in his book *Wild at Heart:*

> For years all my daily energy was spent trying to beat the trials in my life and arrange for a little pleasure. My weeks were wasted away either striving or indulging. I was a mercenary. A mercenary fights for pay, for his own benefit; his life is devoted to himself. "The quality of a true warrior," says [Robert] Bly, "is that he is in service to a purpose greater than himself; that is, to a transcendent cause."[5]

When you grasp—really grasp—that God enlisted you as a solider in an eternal struggle to advance His kingdom throughout the world, you will become much more intentional in every area of your life, from what you eat every day to how you invest your time. Eldredge continues with Bly's explanation of being a warrior:

> When a warrior is in service, however, to a True King—that is, to a transcendent cause—he does well, and his body becomes a hardworking servant which he requires to endure cold, heat, pain, wounds, scarring, hunger, lack of sleep, hardship of all kinds, to do what is necessary.[6]

Just as a soldier in battle or an athlete in competition tames and trains his body to maximize his performance, the Christian who understands his purpose in life will discipline his body to be his slave rather than his master. Think about this for a moment: your body can be either your greatest asset or your greatest liability in serving God.

Your voice can be used to share the gospel with an unbeliever or to discourage another Christian.

Your hands can be used to open God's Word to provide the spiritual food you require, or they can be used to open a magazine or Internet site that will quench your love for God.

Your feet can take you to the front lines of ministry, or they can take you into the Enemy's camp to be seduced and conquered by your opponent.

Your body can be a great tool to achieve or an instrument that destroys your life purpose. This realization prompted Paul to give a word of counsel from his own experience. Paul's greatest fear was that in some unguarded moment he would make a tragic choice that would completely negate his entire ministry. He knew from the strong desires that still raged within him that such a mistake was a strong possibility. His only hope for averting spiritual disaster was to continually ensure that his body was in submission to his spirit:

> Therefore I run in such a way, as not without aim; I box in such a way, as not beating the air; but I discipline my body and make it my slave, so that, after I have preached to others, I myself will not be disqualified. (1 Corinthians 9:26–27)

One of my seminary professors used to advise, "Men, say no to at least one thing you want to do every day just to remind your body who's in charge."

Push away that extra piece of dessert when you would like another.

Turn off the television set when you would like to see an extra episode of your favorite sitcom.

Close *Newsweek* and open your Bible.

Get out of bed thirty minutes earlier on a cold winter morning to spend a few moments with God.

The ability to rule over your body is crucial to fending off Satan's attacks. However, you will never sustain your motivation for self-discipline as long as you live "without aim," as Paul says in 1 Corinthians 9:26. Just as an athlete finds it difficult to train when there is no game on the calendar or a soldier finds it hard to prepare for battle when there's no enemy in sight, Christians without a clearly defined purpose in life will eventually give up on discipline and give in to sin.

Keeping our God-given purpose clearly in focus provides the motivation we all need to live a disciplined life and avoid the traps of the Enemy. It will encourage us to choose purity over immorality, generosity over greed, and diligence over aimlessness.

> Live life, then, with a due sense of responsibility, not as men who do
> not know the meaning and purpose of life but as those who do. Make
> the best use of your time, despite all the difficulties of these days. Don't
> be vague but firmly grasp what you know to be the will of God. (Ephe-
> sians 5:15–17, Phillips)

BOOTING UP FOR SERVICE

We've identified the boots that are foundational to success in spiritual warfare. We've discovered how they help us in our struggle with our enemy. Now let's look at four essential components for centering our lives on God's purpose.

Be convinced of people's need for Christ

Before we will ever risk speaking to someone about Christ, we must first be convinced that he or she really needs Christ. Unfortunately most Christians do not share that conviction. Several years ago, the *Washington Times* ran an article about my book *Hell? Yes!* in which I discuss seven politically incorrect beliefs Christians can articulate in today's world. In response to a chapter titled "Every Other Religion Is Wrong," defending the exclusivity of Christianity, a well-known Jewish rabbi responded:

> Mr. Jeffress is doing his faith a profound disservice. The claim that there is only one way, that all others will go to hell, betrays Christianity. His views are outmoded Christianity that have been disregarded by most of its believers.[7]

The good rabbi is correct on one count: most professing Christians do not believe that faith in Christ is the only way to heaven. According to a poll in *U.S. News & World Report,* only 19 percent of those claiming to be Christians believe that the religion they practice is the only true faith.[8] Do they believe Jesus was lying, or at least exaggerating, in His claim: "I am the way, and the truth, and the life; no one comes to the Father but through Me" (John 14:6)? You will find it difficult to risk rejection by sharing Christ's offer of salvation with a work associate, friend, or family member until you are absolutely convinced that without Christ they are destined for an eternity of separation from God.

Be confident in God's power to save

When you actually grasp the truth that those people around you who die without Christ are destined for an eternity of suffering, you will gain a new boldness in sharing your faith. You will be infused with the kind of courage a firefighter exhibits when he barges into a burning building to save those who are in danger of perishing.

When I was in high school, I heard a sermon titled "Say, Neighbor, Your House Is on Fire." The speaker said that if you were walking by your neighbor's home late one night and saw his house engulfed in flames, you would lay aside your concerns about politeness, bang on his door loudly, scream at the top of your lungs, and, if needed, break into his home to rescue him from the flames.

However, this analogy breaks down in one key respect. The Bible teaches that regardless of how loudly, persuasively, or frequently we attempt to warn a non-Christian of the spiritual danger he faces, there is only one Person who can awaken an unbeliever to the realization of his need for Christ. Jesus said, "No one can come to Me unless the Father who sent Me draws him" (John 6:44). Yes, we are to sound the alarm and point to the way of escape, but only God can awaken someone who is spiritually dead and make him spiritually alive.

Someone once asked the legendary pastor Charles Haddon Spurgeon how he reconciled his evangelistic fervor with his belief that God would only save those He had chosen. In a well-known and oft-repeated story, Spurgeon replied, "If the Lord would paint a yellow stripe down the backs of the elect, then I would walk the streets of London pulling up shirttails. But since He hasn't, I preach the gospel to everyone." You can't save anyone. Only God can perform a spiritual resurrection. That realization removes a lot of unnecessary pressure from evangelism. While we have a responsibility to clearly articulate God's message, ultimately a person's response to the gospel does not depend on our rhetorical skill. We are simply God's mouthpiece through which He voices His invitation.

Be considerate of the unbeliever's level of interest

Much of the evangelism training offered today equips people in confrontational evangelism. The Christian memorizes a canned presentation of the gospel and then scours the landscape for some poor, unsuspecting victim on whom he can unload his spiritual dump truck. While we hear occasional success stories from such an approach, the truth is that very few people respond positively to those kinds of presentations.

Remember Jesus's parable of the soils in Luke? He explained why everyone does not respond to the gospel in the same way. The seed (representing the Word of God) took root in the soft soil. Only a heart that is open and receptive will respond positively to the gospel.

The problem with confrontational evangelism is that it fails to give consideration to a person's level of interest in hearing God's message. In confrontational evangelism, the Christian uses the tactics of a sanctified telephone solicitor who is trained to begin delivering his spiel as soon as the other party answers the phone. How well do you respond when your dinner is interrupted by an uninvited telephone call attempting to sell you a product in which you have no interest? Probably the same way most non-Christians feel when they are forced to listen to a pitch for something in which they have no interest.

In his book *Permission Evangelism*, Michael Simpson encourages Christians to adopt the strategy of a successful salesman who understands the importance of carefully gauging a prospective customer's level of interest in the "product" being offered:

> Every communication must be crafted with the goal of ensuring that it's
> not the last one. The best way to do this is to make sure the potential
> customer knows that he is in charge of choosing how much information
> he receives. He must know you will honor his choice at his level of will-
> ingness to engage, or he will feel pressured and threatened and trust will
> be broken. The goal of "permission evangelism" is to "get them to give
> you more and more permission over time until they say 'I do.'"[9]

Many unbelievers have rejected the gospel, not because of the offensiveness of the message, but because of the offensive approach of some of the messengers.

Comprehend the message

When we do find someone whose heart is receptive toward the gospel, it's important we be able to communicate the basics of God's message. After all, we are His representatives.

> We are ambassadors for Christ, as though God were making an appeal
> through us; we beg you on behalf of Christ, be reconciled to God.
> (2 Corinthians 5:20)

The job of an ambassador in a foreign country is to accurately represent the one who sent him. He is not responsible to craft his own message, but to articulate the policy of the one he represents. As emissaries from heaven living in a foreign land, our task is to voice God's offer of forgiveness to the world. Think about it. The King of heaven has chosen to voice His appeal for reconciliation to mankind through you. Are you equipped to share His offer accurately?

Any presentation of God's message of salvation should contain at least four essential truths:

1. All of us have sinned. "For all have sinned and fall short of the glory of God," states the apostle Paul in Romans 3:23. Sin is disobedience to God's laws, and everyone is guilty of breaking God's laws.

Sometimes I illustrate this truth by asking the listener to imagine three swimmers standing on the shore of California and planning to swim to Hawaii. One swimmer may go ten miles before he sinks, another may be able to swim a hundred miles. The third swimmer may actually swim five hundred miles before succumbing to exhaustion and drowning. Although the third swimmer made it farther than the other two, he still fell short of the goal. Although some people may be better people than others, their relative goodness is inconsequential, because we all fall short of God's glory.

2. We deserve to be punished for our sins. When we were children and broke our parents' rules, we were punished for our disobedience. In the same way, because we have disobeyed God's laws, we deserve His punishment. The Bible declares that "the wages of sin is death" (Romans 6:23). The word *death* not only refers to physical death but to eternal separation from God in hell.

3. Christ died for our sins. This is the essence of the gospel. "But God demonstrates His own love toward us, in that while we were yet sinners, Christ died for us" (Romans 5:8). Jesus Christ willingly took the punishment from God that we deserve for our sins. To explain that truth I occasionally use the illustration of a boy who was arrested for speeding, brought before a judge, and fined two hundred dollars. Since he did not have the money to pay the fine, the judge sentenced him to thirty days in jail. But then the judge did something unusual. He stood up, removed his judicial robe, stepped down from the bench, went to the bailiff, and paid the fine himself. Why? The judge was also the boy's father.

In some inexplicable way, the same God whose holy nature demands a payment for sin also paid the necessary fine for our sin by taking off His heavenly robe, assuming the role of a servant, and paying the penalty for our disobedience through His death on the cross.

4. We must receive God's gift of forgiveness. A gift is not a gift unless it is received. Several years ago, talk-show host Oprah Winfrey surprised her studio audience by giving everyone a new automobile. They were overwhelmed by her generosity until they discovered that with the gift came an obligation requiring over $7,500 in gift taxes. Some audience members, unable to come up with the money, escaped the tax bill by refusing the car. The Internal Revenue Service says a gift that is not received is not a gift.

Similarly, only those who actually receive God's gift of forgiveness benefit from His gift. John 1:12 says, "As many as *received* Him, to them He gave the right to become children of God, even to those who believe in His name." At this point in my conversation with an unbeliever, I usually ask if he understands what I've been saying. After answering any questions, I then ask, "Would you like to receive God's gift of forgiveness right now?" If he responds positively—giving me permission to continue—I invite him to repeat the following prayer after me:

> Dear God,
>
>   I know that I have disappointed You in so many ways, and I am truly sorry for my sins. But I believe that You sent Jesus to die on the cross for me. Right now I am trusting in Jesus to save me from my sins. Thank You for forgiving me and help me to live for You. In Jesus's name, I pray.

If the person says no to your invitation, you can ask if anything you said is unclear. If he is still reluctant, graciously thank him for listening to you, assure him of your continued prayers, and encourage him to contact you if you can be of assistance in the future. By demonstrating sensitivity to your listener's level of interest, you are keeping the door open to future communication.

Over the past months, our family has been attempting to lead a family friend to faith in Christ. I'll confess that at times I have felt pressured to dump the whole load on him without consideration of his level of interest, which was obviously low. However, I resisted that impulse and instead prayed for him every day as we looked for openings in our conversations to talk with him about Christ.

Last night that opening occurred, and I led him in the prayer I suggested to you. When I went to bed, I was more excited about having led that young man to Christ than about any sermon I've delivered or any book I've written. It was as if God said to me, "Robert, *this* is the reason you are here."

It is also the reason *you* are here rather than in heaven at this very moment. J. Campbell White observed:

> Most [people] are not satisfied with the permanent output of their
> lives. Nothing can wholly satisfy the life of Christ within his followers
> except the adoption of Christ's purpose toward the world he came to
> redeem. Fame, pleasure, and riches are but husks and ashes in contrast
> with the boundless and abiding joy of working with God for the fulfill-
> ment of his eternal plans. The [people] who are putting everything into
> Christ's undertakings are getting out of life its sweetest and most price-
> less rewards.[10]

I pray that you will discover the same pleasure and spiritual power that come from adopting God's purpose as your purpose.

STORMING THE GATES OF HELL

Strategy 4: Move forward in spite of your doubts

Strategy 5: Remember your power to win

Strategy 6: Strengthen your resolve to resist

> My orders are to fight; then if I bleed, or fail, or
> strongly win, what matters it?… I was not told to win
> or lose, my orders are to fight.
> —ETHELWYN WETHERALD

One of the truisms of football is applicable to your war with Satan and his demons: the best defense is a good offense. When a soldier hears the bullets zinging and the bombs bursting overhead, his first response is to hit the ground to protect himself from injury. While such a reaction is natural and necessary, it is not sufficient to win the battle. Eventually the soldier must get up, move forward, and put the enemy on the defensive.

A few months after our country's invasion of Iraq, a friend of mine had dinner at the White House with President George W. Bush. At that time, the commander in chief was under heavy criticism for waging a war that was costing hundreds of billions of dollars and might result in thousands of casualties. The president explained to my friend his rationale for the war. "As long as we have the terrorists on the defensive, they are less likely to go on the offensive."

God wants you to do more than simply hunker down and do the best you can to deflect Satan's attacks. To avoid becoming a casualty of war is not enough. God invites you to join Him in His march against Satan and his kingdom of darkness.

In describing the power of the church, Jesus said, "Upon this rock I will build My church; and the gates of Hades will not overpower it" (Matthew 16:18). Notice that in Jesus's vivid imagery, it is not the church that is hiding behind the gates, trying to survive Satan's battering ram. It is just the opposite. Jesus pictures Satan and his forces of darkness cowering in fear behind the gates of their kingdom, attempting to defend it against the invading church as we reclaim the world they have taken hostage. The fortress Satan has erected around this world is formidable, but it is no match for the spiritual firepower of Jesus and His followers.

Christians represent the first wave of forces God has sent to infiltrate this world and soften it up before our Commander returns for the final assault and reclamation of what is rightfully His.

Every time you lead someone to become a Christian, you have helped to rescue a person from the Enemy's camp and released Satan's grip on this world a little more.

Every time you speak an affirming word to another Christian, you encourage one of our own troops, giving him strength to continue the fight.

Every time you give glory to God for something He has done in your life, you help break the spell the Enemy has cast over those under his control.

Every time you refuse to surrender any area of your life to Satan, you thwart his plan and throw him into chaos.

I need to clarify what I mean by fighting Satan offensively. I'm not suggesting that we engage in "binding" Satan (something Christians are never commanded to do), casting out demonic spirits (a questionable practice), or challenging satanic forces to some kind of spiritual duel. Being on the offensive simply means moving forward rather than stopping or retreating as you walk along the unique path God has designed for your life.

The Word of God continually employs the metaphor of walking or sometimes running (when the biblical writers were feeling especially energetic) to describe our life on earth:

Therefore I, the prisoner of the Lord, implore you to *walk* in a manner worthy of the calling with which you have been called. (Ephesians 4:1)

For this reason also, since the day we heard of it, we have not ceased to pray for you and to ask that you may be filled with the knowledge of His will in all spiritual wisdom and understanding, so that you will *walk* in a manner worthy of the Lord, to please Him in all respects, bearing fruit in every good work and increasing in the knowledge of God. (Colossians 1:9–10)

Walk in a manner worthy of the God who calls you into His own kingdom and glory. (1 Thessalonians 2:12)

Let us run with endurance the race that is set before us, fixing our eyes on Jesus, the author and perfecter of faith. (Hebrews 12:1–2)

The idea of walking or running pictures you moving forward to complete God's unique plan for your life. However, you have an Enemy who realizes that your moving forward in God's plan will result in his moving backward in his own plan! Therefore, Satan's goal is to stop you from advancing, even though he lacks the authority to do so.

Picture yourself standing at the end of a long, narrow street that is lined on each side by rows of two-story apartment buildings. At the other end of the street, Jesus Christ is calling you to come toward Him. The street represents the course of your life as you move toward the Author and Finisher of your faith, Jesus Christ. While there is no obstacle in the street actually preventing you from moving forward toward the finish line, there are demonic inhabitants hanging out the windows of those apartment buildings who try to discourage or distract you from walking toward Jesus. Although they have no real power over you, they act as if they do.

Sometimes the demons' tactic is to discourage you. From their windows they shout out, "You're too weak to make it to the finish line, why even try?" Other times they attempt to distract you with appealing enticements. "Aren't you tired of being lonely and unsatisfied? Come in here with us and enjoy what we have to offer," they plead. Still others will attempt to deceive you by saying, "The path you are on won't get you to God. You need a new way to God since that path isn't getting you where you really want to go."

While the taunts are varied, the goal is the same. Satan and his forces want to slow you down or stop you from moving ahead. Every step forward you take represents one more nail in their coffins. Remember, they have no power over you, but they want you to believe they do. The key to success is to keep moving forward.[1]

In addition to the pieces of spiritual armor we've discussed previously, Paul mentions three others that will help you do more than simply hold your ground and defend yourself. These three pieces of armor are the keys to moving forward and going on the offensive along the unique life course God has set before you.

THE SHIELD OF FAITH: MOVE FORWARD IN SPITE OF YOUR DOUBTS

Last night I was watching an episode of *24*, the high-action TV drama in which the lead character is always fighting terrorists who are plotting to destroy the world. In this particular episode, the bad guys were holed up in a house with some terrified hostages. The hero stood outside, strategizing how to handle the situation. Finally, he said to the SWAT team, "Hand me the shield." Once he had the protective piece of armor in hand, he barged into the home in spite of the barrage of bullets from the terrorists, saving the day once again. The shield was instrumental in his ability to move forward, act on the offensive, and claim victory.

Similarly, Paul says that a key to advancing in God's plan for our lives is:

[Take] up the shield of faith with which you will be able to extinguish all the flaming arrows of the evil one. (Ephesians 6:16)

The Roman shield was a piece of wood, four and one-half feet long and about two and one-half feet wide. The wooden shield was covered with leather that had been soaked in water. The enemy would shoot arrows that had been dipped in pitch and set on fire. The closer a soldier marched toward enemy front lines, the more intense the barrage of flaming arrows. But when those flaming missiles struck the water-soaked leather shield, they were immediately extinguished.

Likewise, while we need to always be on guard against Satan's attacks, the more progress you make in fulfilling God's plan for your life, the more intense the barrage of flaming arrows you can expect. It is during those most concentrated times of attack that you need to raise the shield of faith for protection.

To understand what Paul has in mind, let's look again at the word *faith*. Today some people are teaching that exercising faith means conjuring up a positive feeling that what we want to happen will actually happen:

- If we have enough faith that we will get the promotion, we will get the promotion.
- If we have enough faith that God will heal our sickness, He will heal our sickness.
- If we have enough faith that our marriage will be saved, our marriage will be saved.

In this sense, faith is little more than transforming ourselves into the Little Engine That Could as we chug along, chanting, "I think I can, I think I can, I think I can."

But the Bible offers a much different definition of faith:

Faith is the *assurance* of things hoped for, the *conviction* of things not
seen. (Hebrews 11:1)

Faith is not a synonym for hope, wish or desire. Faith is defined as an
assurance. The word translated *assurance* refers to the concrete foundation
under a pillar. Faith is the absolute, concrete assurance that God will do what
He promised to do. God has not promised to grant every request for a promotion, heal every disease (not in this life, anyway!), or restore every marriage.
But the Bible is filled with universal and eternal truths about God and with
promises from God on which we can build our lives.

The word *conviction* refers to behavior that is the result of an unshakable
faith in God's promises. The remainder of Hebrews 11 is devoted to examples
of men and women who believed that God's promises would prevail and acted
accordingly.

- Noah believed God's promise to destroy the world by a flood, so he
  built a boat.
- Abraham believed God's promise to make him the father of a great
  nation, so he packed up his tent and moved to an unknown land.
- Rahab the harlot believed God's promise to favor Israel over the
  Canaanites, so she risked her life to help the two Jewish spies.

Here's a simple definition of faith: having faith is to believe that God will
do what He has promised to do and then to act accordingly.

Genuine faith is proved by obedience to God's commands, even when
that obedience makes little sense. In relationship to spiritual warfare, holding
up the shield of faith means moving forward in obedience to God, even when
Satan attempts to stop you dead in your tracks with his flaming arrows of
doubt, discouragement, or disobedience.

Consider the story of Job, a man who endured more than his fair share of
Satan's flaming missiles. In a short period of time, Job lost his possessions, his
children, and his health—all because Satan was trying to turn Job's allegiance

away from God. Although at times Job voiced the same questions we all have about suffering, he reminded himself (and all of us) of three eternal, often-hidden truths about God, and he acted accordingly.

God is in control—trust Him

This world in general, and our worlds in particular, frequently appears out of control. Satan takes advantage of our limited perspective and taunts us in our lowest moments. "If there really is a God, why would he take your child from you, allow your mate to desert you, or permit this illness to strike you?" he asks. "Maybe God is angry with you or is incapable of helping, or maybe he doesn't even exist. Whatever the case, he certainly is not worthy of your devotion. You had better start looking out for yourself."

Satan voiced those same doubts to Job through Job's wife and friends. Yet even though Job did not understand God's plan, he still trusted in God's power. "I know that You can do all things, and that no purpose of Yours can be thwarted" (Job 42:2). Taking up the shield of faith means trusting that God has a plan He is working out in your life, even when the darkness hides that plan from you.

God rewards the righteous—obey Him

This is another one of those unseen truths that requires faith to believe and faith to act on. It's difficult to say no to momentary pleasures of sin that everyone else seems to be enjoying when there appears to be no visible benefit in doing so. It *appears* that the righteous and unrighteous experience the same fates: everyone gets sick, everyone has family difficulties, and everyone dies. Where, then, is the upside in obeying God?

At one point Job lamented, "How often is the lamp of the wicked put out, or does their calamity fall on them?" (Job 21:17). In other words, Job was wondering, *If evil people were supposed to suffer, why doesn't it appear they ever do?*

Yet in spite of his understandable doubts, and even when all the evidence argued otherwise, Job still believed God would eventually reward his obedience. The New Testament writer James encourages us to imitate the endurance of Job and reminds us that God did eventually reward his faithful servant (see James 5:11). When Satan launches his arrows of temptation, we must believe that obedience to God's commands will eventually be rewarded, even when all visible evidence is to the contrary.

God's kingdom will prevail—serve Him

"I would rather fail in a cause that will ultimately succeed than succeed in a cause that will ultimately fail," said Abraham Lincoln. One motivation to keep moving forward in our service to God is the realization that ultimately He *is* going to defeat Satan's kingdom of darkness. It only makes sense to want to be on the winning side when the conflict ends!

Believing that God's kingdom will eventually prevail requires faith since most of the visible evidence suggests otherwise. Skim the front page of today's newspaper or survey the surrounding landscape of your own world; it appears that evil is winning over good.

Job could have easily arrived at the same conclusion. From the losses he sustained, Job had every reason to doubt God's power to triumph over Satan. Yet even when Satan appeared to be firmly in control of the entire world, Job declared, "I know that my Redeemer lives, and at the last He will take His stand on the earth. Even after my skin is destroyed, yet from my flesh I shall see God" (Job 19:25–26). Job chose to continue serving God even when God appeared to be on the losing side.

In this war between God and Satan, there is no room for neutrality. You must decide whether you are going to serve God or Satan. There is no middle ground. Holding up the shield of faith provides the confidence that you are on the winning side and the courage to move forward.

THE HELMET OF SALVATION: REMEMBER YOUR POWER TO WIN

A few days ago I participated in a question-and-answer session with our men's ministry group. One of the participants asked, "Pastor, what is the hardest thing you have ever had to do in ministry?" I didn't have to think long because my most difficult experience is seared into my memory. On a Palm Sunday afternoon several years ago, just an hour before the church Easter pageant, I received word that a couple in our church had been killed in a motorcycle accident. The extended family requested that I go to the couple's home and tell their two grade-school daughters that their parents were dead. Trust me, it doesn't get any harder than that. If only the couple had been wearing helmets, their deaths, and the resulting grief inflicted on their families, might have been prevented. Helmets are vital to survival in motorcycling—and in warfare.

And take the helmet of salvation. (Ephesians 6:17)

In Paul's day, a Roman soldier would never think of advancing toward the enemy without a helmet. The Roman helmet was made of strong molded metal and fashioned with plates to guard the face. The purpose of the helmet was to protect the soldier's head from a mortal wound inflicted in any number of ways.

If the soldier were on foot, the helmet might save him from an enemy on horseback flailing the long broadsword you often see in movies. In hand-to-hand combat, the helmet was a powerful defense against the blows of daggers, clubs, and chains. Occasionally, the helmet might even protect the soldier from himself if he accidentally stumbled on a rock or fell off his horse.

In spiritual warfare, the helmet of salvation serves to protect your mind from the mortal blows of the Adversary. As we saw previously, the mind is command central. Every choice you make begins with a thought. No wonder that your mind is a primary target for Satan's attacks.

What does it mean to put on the helmet of salvation, especially if you are already a Christian? Most Bible commentaries suggest Paul uses the helmet as a symbol of the assurance of salvation. One of Satan's most effective attacks against Christians causes us to doubt that the salvation promised really belongs to us. That's why we must continually remind ourselves of what we have received from Christ.

We have salvation from the penalty of sin

In our church we have many people who join from a variety of denominations. One of the questions I'm most frequently asked in our new members' class is this: "What about this 'once saved always saved' idea you Baptists teach? If I really believed that, what would keep me from sinning all I wanted to?"

Such a question fails to account for the radical change in desire that occurs when we are born again. Becoming a Christian doesn't mean we will never sin; it just means we won't enjoy sinning as much as we used to. But the question also assumes we need the fear of losing our salvation to keep us close to God.

In reality, fear does not promote intimacy; it inhibits it. Suppose your spouse were always threatening to leave you. Five extra pounds gained, two socks not picked up, or one careless word spoken in anger, and out the door he goes. Under those circumstances, what kind of true intimacy could you achieve with your mate? You would carefully guard your words and conceal any thoughts or actions your mate might disapprove of.

God loves us with a perfect love, a love that casts out all fear (see 1 John 4:18). He desires that we share every aspect of our lives with Him. Such freedom of exchange is only possible when we feel absolutely secure in His love. Jesus offers us that security:

> My sheep hear My voice, and I know them, and they follow Me; and
> I give *eternal* life to them, and they will *never perish*; and no one will
> snatch them out of My hand. (John 10:27–28)

Our salvation is eternal, not temporary, Jesus promises. We never need to fear perishing. No one—not Satan, not another person, not even we ourselves—can pry us loose from our Father's grip! As someone has said, "If after trusting in Christ for my salvation I still go to hell, I will have lost my soul," someone said, "but God will have lost His character, reputation, and good name."

But there is another aspect of our salvation about which we must be equally assured if we are going to move forward in our advance against the Enemy.

We have salvation from the power of sin

"You have no choice, you must give in," the Enemy declares as his flaming arrows zoom toward us. Sometimes that lie comes from a TV sitcom or a book suggesting it's abnormal, and even harmful, not to surrender to our natural desires.

Other times, well-meaning but misinformed counselors tell us that venting our anger or refusing to unconditionally forgive others is permissible behavior since we're "only human." Occasionally, the lie is voiced through other Christians who assume disobedience is inevitable because our sin nature remains with us even after we become Christians. They sigh, "Not until we get to heaven will we experience victory over sin."

Regardless of the instrument Satan uses, the lie that we are prisoners of sin is lethal to our success in spiritual warfare. If defeat is unavoidable, then why bother to put up a fight?

But the Word of God assures us salvation is not only for the hereafter but also for the here and now. The same power that raised Jesus from the dead—and will one day resurrect our bodies from the grave—is alive and working in our lives right now, offering us freedom from the power of sin. As Paul reminded the Roman Christians: "The power of the life-giving Spirit has freed you from the power of sin that leads to death" (Romans 8:2, NLT).

Let me offer a practical way you can put on the helmet of salvation whenever the Enemy tries to convince you disobedience is your only option. By memorizing and meditating regularly on Romans 6:11–13, you will saturate your mind with the truth about your salvation from the power of sin:

Even so consider yourselves to be dead to sin, but alive to God in
Christ Jesus.

Therefore do not let sin reign in your mortal body so that you
obey its lusts, and do not go on presenting the members of your body
to sin as instruments of unrighteousness; but present yourselves to God
as those alive from the dead, and your members as instruments of
righteousness to God.

The assurance that you have been delivered from both the penalty and the
power of sin provides you with a powerful advantage over the Enemy.

THE SWORD OF THE SPIRIT: STRENGTHEN YOUR RESOLVE TO RESIST

The final piece of armor Paul describes in Ephesians 6 is "the sword of the
Spirit" (verse 17). The Greek word Paul uses for "sword" is *machaira*, referring
to a dagger between six and eighteen inches long rather than the unwieldy
Roman broadsword. The dagger was only useful in hand-to-hand combat and
required a great amount of skill to use effectively.

The writer of Hebrews describes God's Word as "living and active and
sharper than any two-edged sword" (Hebrews 4:12). We don't have to wonder what Paul had in mind when he spoke of the sword of the Spirit. The
apostle clearly identified a Christian's dagger as the Word of God. Like the
machaira, the Bible can be lethal to our enemy. The writer of Hebrews continues in verse 12 saying,

[The Word of God is] able to judge the thoughts and intentions of
the heart.

The power of the Bible is not so much in what it does *to* Satan but in what
it does *for* us. The Word of God has the ability to cut through the fog of Satan's
deceptions that may have descended upon our minds so that we can clearly

see God's truth. In chapter 5 we discussed how Satan attempts to direct our actions by seizing control of our thoughts. When he plants destructive ideas in our minds, we must recognize and replace those harmful thoughts with God's eternal truths.

To do that, we must know which of God's truths will serve as antidotes to Satan's lies. Like the Roman dagger, the Bible must be used skillfully if it is to be effective in spiritual warfare. That means knowing precisely which passages of Scripture to pull out of the sheath when we face specific temptations. If I'm sitting in front of a computer screen wrestling with whether or not to click on an Internet site I know is filled with immorality, recalling Leviticus 13:40 is not going to be of much help to me: "Now if a man loses the hair of his head, he is bald; he is clean." While those words are certainly God's words, they are not particularly useful to me in fending off Satan's attack at that moment.

Let's return for a moment to Luke 4 and Jesus's encounter with Satan in the wilderness. When Satan tempted the Lord with thoughts of discontent, Jesus responded by quoting a verse from the Old Testament about God's sufficiency to satisfy our deepest cravings (verse 4). When Satan enticed the Lord with thoughts of power and riches, Jesus responded by reciting God's greatest commandment: "You shall worship the Lord your God and serve Him only" (verse 8). When Satan tempted Jesus to act independently from God, Jesus responded by quoting the Old Testament admonition to "not put the Lord your God to the test" (verse 12).

Finally, "When the devil had finished every temptation, he left Him until an opportune time" (verse 13). What caused Satan to give up and leave Jesus alone?

I used to believe—and teach—that it was Jesus's quotation of Scripture that sent Satan running for the hills, much like the old TV commercials for the bug killer Raid. Are you old enough to remember those animated classics? A group of cartoon insects would be wreaking havoc in a home when a can of Raid would suddenly appear. The terrified insects would scream "Raid!" as they ran for their lives.

I used to mentally replay that commercial when I read the story of Jesus's encounter with Satan in the desert. I would picture Satan taunting the Lord with those ungodly thoughts and Jesus responding by spraying a Bible verse on Satan, with the devil yelling, "The Word of God!" as he retreated under some rock.

But the more I read the Luke passage, the more I understand that Jesus's reason for quoting Scripture when tempted was for His own benefit, not for Satan's destruction. The devil is certainly not afraid of the Bible. In fact, he knows the Word of God better than most believers, and he actually quoted it back to Jesus during this encounter in the desert. Jesus understood that the best way to dismiss an unwelcome thought is to replace it with another, more-powerful thought. The best way to dispel darkness is to confront it with light! Only when Satan realized he was getting nowhere with Jesus did he retreat, at least temporarily, until a better opportunity arose.

The power of the Word of God is in what it does for us, not in what it does to Satan. Scripture is a powerful weapon that helps us slice through the fog of Satan's lies. The Bible provides us with the discernment to recognize Satan's deceptions so that we have the power to say, "Thanks, but no thanks." It is our consistent resistance to Satan's offers that eventually causes him (or his demons) to depart. "Resist the devil and he will flee from you" (James 4:7).

My friend and former seminary professor Howard Hendricks used to point out that Jesus responded to each of Satan's temptations by quoting from three relatively obscure passages from the Old Testament book of Deuteronomy. Prof would ask, "If your spiritual survival depended on how well you knew the book of Deuteronomy, how long would you last?" And then he would add, "Perhaps that is why you are not any more successful than you are in fending off the Enemy's attack."

Hendricks's words hit me just as hard today as they did nearly thirty years ago when I first heard them. The ability to use God's Word skillfully is not optional; it is essential for success in spiritual warfare.

"The test of a person's character is what it takes to stop him," someone once said. Make no mistake about it. Satan has a well-crafted plan to stop you dead in your tracks in your pursuit of God's plan for your life. But God has provided you with the spiritual equipment you need to move forward in spite of the flaming arrows the devil launches in your direction:

- the certainty of God's promises
- the assurance of God's salvation
- the power of God's Word

Against such weaponry, your Enemy doesn't have a prayer.

PART THREE

LIVING THE DIVINE
DEFENSE

Exercise Power or Exorcise Demons?

Beware of the weird

> When we are fighting with the forces
> of evil, it is actually a mop-up operation....
> Satan is basically on the run.
> —M. Scott Peck

On a gray February afternoon as I walked out of the church I was serving in downtown Dallas, a street person looking for a handout approached me. I'd learned through the years how to dismiss these people with a smile and a "wish I could help but...," reasoning to myself that any money given would only be used to indulge their particular addiction. But there was something different about this individual. His flashing eyes and incoherent speech appeared to be more than a drunken rant.

As I attempted to converse with him, a church member named Ira rounded the corner, quickly assessed the situation, and decided to help. Ira was considered eccentric by a large number of our congregation. He always sat on the front row of our services and yelled "Amen" at some of the most inappropriate moments. One such instance occurred when the pastor declared that two hundred thousand teenage girls had become pregnant the previous year, inciting Ira to shout at the top of his lungs, "Amen!"

In spite of his eccentricities, Ira was a fervent prayer warrior who consistently shared his faith with others and who possessed a unique spiritual sensitivity I have rarely witnessed. As I stumbled through a canned gospel presentation I had memorized, Ira stood by silently praying. After a few moments, Ira opened his eyes and said, "Brother Robert, would you mind if I prayed for this man?"

I gladly yielded the spiritual reins to Ira. He then began to pray for the man, sprinkling his prayer with frequent mentions of the name of Jesus Christ and references to the blood of Jesus.

Every time Ira said anything about Jesus Christ, His blood, or the cross, the man began to yell at the top of his lungs. Ira never missed a beat. As Ira's voice rose, the man dropped to the ground and began rolling over and over. Ira prayed even more fervently and concluded his prayer by saying, "In the name of Jesus I command this demon to depart!" Suddenly, the man became still and quiet.

After a few moments, the man stood up, dusted himself off, thanked us for the help, and walked away. My eyes were as big as his had been a few moments earlier. In my twenty-five years of living, I had never witnessed anything like that! Ira watched the man leave, looked at me, and in a matter-of-fact tone said, "Demon possession. See it all the time." With that observation, Ira turned and continued walking down the sidewalk. Another day, another demon. No big deal!

Twenty-five years later, I still look back on that encounter and wonder if I witnessed a supernatural deliverance from demonic possession. Even if the experience were legitimate, did it guarantee the man's protection from future demonic control? Is this the method every Christian should use to experience freedom from demonic influence?

Perhaps you've never had a close encounter with exorcism, the freeing of an individual from an evil spirit. Nevertheless, movies like *The Exorcist,* TV documentaries, or news accounts of Christians using prayers and religious incantations to rid an individual of demonic control may have made you wonder what role exorcisms should play in spiritual warfare.

Are there extreme cases of demonic influence that require extreme practices like exorcism?

Do Christians possess the power to free other individuals from satanic control?

Given the biblical accounts of exorcism, why don't we use this practice more today?

Is there a more-effective way than exorcism to free an individual from demonic control?

Meet the First Exorcist

I recall a comment by a British pastor who lamented, "When the apostle Paul preached, the people rioted. After I preach, my people have tea." When Jesus preached, He not only excited the people, He also incited the demons. The first occurrence of an exorcism in the Bible is found in Luke 4, during the early days of Jesus's earthly ministry:

> And He [Jesus] came down to Capernaum, a city of Galilee, and He
> was teaching them on the Sabbath; and they were amazed at His teach-
> ing, for His message was with authority. In the synagogue there was a
> man possessed by the spirit of an unclean demon, and he cried out
> with a loud voice, "Let us alone! What business do we have with each
> other, Jesus of Nazareth? Have You come to destroy us? I know who
> You are—the Holy One of God!" (Luke 4:31–34)

As we saw in chapter 4, demons are more than crude first-century at-
tempts to explain the existence of evil or the reality of mental illness. If demons are not real beings, and yet Jesus conversed with them, then Jesus must have been delusional!

Furthermore, demons have intelligence; this particular demon recognized Jesus as the Son of God. Demons have emotions; this one feared what Jesus would do to him and his cohorts. Demons have wills; this minion of Satan chose to submit to Jesus's authority.

But Jesus rebuked him, saying, "Be quiet and come out of him!"
And when the demon had thrown him down in the midst of
the people, he came out of him without doing him any harm.
(Luke 4:35)

Notice the method Jesus employed to exorcise the demon from this individual. Jesus didn't rant and rave at the demonic spirit, reminding him that He was the boss! He did not ask His apostles to form a circle around the individual and spend hours praying for his release from spiritual oppression. He did not use incense, garlic, and Latin incantations to free the demon-possessed individual.

Jesus simply said, "Be quiet" (literally, "be muzzled," or as we might say today, "Put a lid on it!") "and come out of him." No pleading, no arguing about who was in charge, no rituals. Just a simple command. And the demon complied.

Isn't it interesting that even demons recognize Christ's authority over them? Of all the occupants of God's vast creation—the angels, the saints in heaven, the unbelievers in hades, the demons on earth and under the earth, and even Satan himself—the only creatures who do not recognize the complete authority of Jesus Christ are those human beings who have not yet surrendered to Him. Even that rebellion will be short-lived:

At the name of Jesus every knee will bow, of those who are in heaven
and on earth and under the earth, and…every tongue will confess
that Jesus Christ is Lord, to the glory of God the Father. (Philippians
2:10–11)

DELEGATED AUTHORITY

Jesus also gave His twelve apostles the power to cast out demons from possessed individuals as well as to heal every kind of sickness.

> Jesus summoned His twelve disciples and gave them authority over
> unclean spirits, to cast them out, and to heal every kind of disease and
> every kind of sickness. (Matthew 10:1)

The apostles' ability to perform miraculous feats would authenticate their
message that Jesus Christ was the long-awaited Messiah. But this supernatural
power to heal the diseased and exorcise the demon possessed was clearly limited to the apostles. Matthew emphasizes that point by listing the names of the
twelve who were given this unique power.

> Now the names of the twelve apostles are these: The first, Simon, who is
> called Peter, and Andrew his brother; and James the son of Zebedee, and
> John his brother; Philip and Bartholomew; Thomas and Matthew the tax
> collector; James the son of Alphaeus, and Thaddaeus; Simon the Zealot,
> and Judas Iscariot, the one who betrayed Him. (Matthew 10:2–4)

Has this power been extended to Christians today? Do we have the same
ability to cast out demons that Jesus and the apostles possessed? Could it be that
one reason we are not enjoying more success in our struggle against Satan is our
failure to utilize this important weapon against the kingdom of darkness?

Please note, I believe Christians can today *experience* healing from disease
and *experience* freedom from demonic influence. It is the power to *grant* healing and deliverance from demons to others that was limited to the apostles.

The Limitations of Exorcism

I want to suggest three reasons why exorcism, as practiced in the New Testament, is neither a relevant nor even an effective tool for believers today.

The gift is attached to specific individuals

Clearly, Jesus had the ability to exorcise demons. As we saw in Matthew 10,
Jesus also empowered the twelve apostles to cast out demons. But go back and

carefully read Matthew 10:2–4. Do you find the name of any prominent tel-evangelist in that list? Do you find *your* name in that list? Why do so many believers assume that a power given to twelve specifically named individuals has been passed on to us?

Suppose you received a copy of the following memo at work:

To: Division Managers James Rubin, Jerry Gillam, John Newhouse
From: Tim Roberts, President

This is to confirm that I have given you the authority to each hire an assistant at a salary not to exceed $50,000.

You are not one of the three division managers to whom the memo is addressed, but feeling a little overworked yourself, you go out and hire an assis-tant to provide some relief. The only problem is this: you simply received a copy of the memo to keep you abreast of what was happening in the company. How would your supervisor respond to your hiring an assistant without the proper authorization?

"Well, I just assumed because those three men had the authority to hire someone, I could too," you respond. "After all, I'm part of the corporation." Most likely your employer would remind you that this authority was given only to the division managers, not to you.

While it is true that all of the Bible was written *for* us, not all of it was written *to* us. God has not commanded you to build an ark like He did Noah, to sacrifice your firstborn son like He did Abraham, or to march around the walls of Jericho blowing a trumpet as He did Joshua. Those commands to spe-cific individuals are recorded in the Scriptures for our benefit to teach us some important lessons about God.

Every command and every promise in the Bible needs to be read in con-text, especially commands and promises that are addressed to specific individ-uals or groups. In Matthew 10 the authority to cast out demons and heal the sick was given to a distinct group of individuals.

Note: There is one passage in the Bible that appears to teach that every Christian has been given the ability to exorcise demons.

> These signs will accompany those who have believed: in My name they
> will cast out demons, they will speak with new tongues; they will pick
> up serpents, and if they drink any deadly poison, it will not hurt them;
> they will lay hands on the sick, and they will recover. (Mark 16:17–18)

Most study Bibles place Mark 16:9–20 in brackets with a note explaining that two of the most reliable New Testament manuscripts do not contain these verses. As noted scholar Dr. Charles Ryrie says, "The doubtful genuineness of verses 9–20 makes it unwise to build a doctrine or base an experience on them."[1]

It is probably not wise to drink poison, pick up a snake, or attempt an exorcism based on these two verses. The fact that the overwhelming majority of believers do not have the power to heal the sick or to survive a lethal dose of venom suggests that they also lack the power to cast out demons since that power is placed on equal footing with these other miraculous gifts. Except for this one, highly questionable passage, no other passage in the Bible teaches that the power of exorcism has been given to anyone except Jesus, the apostles, and several men associated with the apostles in the book of Acts.

The gift is infrequently mentioned

If exorcism is an important weapon for Christians to use in their battle against Satan, why don't Paul, Peter, and John ever refer to it in their instructions to the church? After the book of Acts, which records the ministry of the apostles—most notably Peter and Paul (selected by Christ Himself)—there is not one mention of exorcism in the remainder of the Bible.

I remember from my argumentation-and-debate class in college that the argument from silence is one of the weakest arguments there is. Just because something is not mentioned does not prove it does not exist. Nevertheless, in all the instructions about the operation of the church (1 Corinthians), the listing of spiritual gifts (Romans 12), pastoral advice from Paul (1 and 2 Timothy), or the listing of weapons for spiritual warfare (Ephesians 6), there is no command concerning, or even reference to, the exorcism of demonic spirits. I believe this makes the practice highly questionable for the church today.

The gift has limited effectiveness across time

Our desire for efficiency attracts us to simple answers for complex problems. We begin the diet that promises to end our battle with the bulge. We buy the book or attend the seminar that promises to restore intimacy to our marriage. We pray the prayer we hope will free us from the addiction that is destroying us.

It is no surprise that we would be drawn to the possibility of a religious ritual that could release us, or someone we love, once and for all from Satan's stranglehold. Suppose your mate suffers from severe depression or one of your children is addicted to drugs. Years of counseling and medication have not alleviated the problem. You are desperate for some relief. If someone suggested that your family member was being held captive by a demonic influence and could be freed from it by participating in a spiritual exercise, wouldn't you at least be open to that possibility?

But here is the downside to exorcisms that is rarely discussed: they don't last. Even if a priest, pastor, or group of spiritual friends had the power to cast out the demon from your loved one, what would prevent that demon from invading your loved one's life again? Jesus raised that very real possibility:

> When the unclean spirit goes out of a man, it passes through waterless places seeking rest, and not finding any, it says, "I will return to my house from which I came." And when it comes, it finds it swept and put in order. Then it goes and takes along seven other spirits more evil than itself, and they go in and live there; and the last state of that man becomes worse than the first. (Luke 11:24–26)

Theologians differ on the spiritual condition of the man Jesus envisions here. Is he an unbeliever who is still in Satan's possession? Or is he a believer who has allowed a particular area of his life to become demonized because he failed to yield complete control of his life to God?

In either case, Jesus explains that there is no one-time ritual like exorcism that demon-proofs your life forever. If a demonic spirit can invade someone's life once (either through possession of a non-Christian or influence over a Christian), then it can do so again.

Dr. M. Scott Peck believes that the key to understanding both demonic possession (or, for Christians, demonic influence) and exorcism is the human will. In his book *Glimpses of the Devil*, Peck describes, from a medical doctor's perspective, two accounts of demon possession and exorcism.

Although I don't agree with all of Peck's conclusions, he makes one observation that I believe is dead-on accurate: the single most important factor in demonic control is a person's choices. In one example, Peck traces a woman's demonic possession to an evil book that fascinated her as a little girl. Peck believes that there is always an act of the will that opens a person to demonic possession or influence.[2]

Likewise, Peck believes that the most important factor in a person's deliverance from demonic control is the person's desire to be freed. In an interview with *Christianity Today*, Peck observed, "There are four exorcists. The most important, the one who determines whether exorcism succeeds or not, is the patient himself or herself."[3]

Perhaps Peck's observations explain why there is no mention of exorcisms in the New Testament after the book of Acts. The purpose of exorcisms during the days of Jesus's and His apostles' ministries was to authenticate their authority and validate their message. It was not to provide a once-for-all deliverance for the demon possessed (just as those who were healed from sickness were not exempted from further illnesses or death).

While there is no longer a need to authenticate Jesus's or the apostles' authority and message, there *is* a need for believers to continually lead lives that are free of satanic influence. As Neil Anderson writes, "The responsibility for living free in Christ has shifted from the specially endowed agent of authority to the individual believer."[4]

Instead of depending upon others to exorcise demons, we are responsible for exercising God's power to win the spiritual battle in which we are engaged. Nowhere does Scripture command Christians to bind Satan or cast out demons. However, in James, we are told to "resist the devil" with the promise that "he will flee from you" (4:7).

In the next chapter we will discover six practical ways you can resist the devil before he destroys you.

Using the Divine Defense

Six effective ways to keep Satan on the run

> If we would endeavor, like men of courage,
> to stand in the battle, surely we would feel
> the favorable assistance of God from heaven.
> — Thomas à Kempis

I realize that some of you reading this book may disagree with statements made in the previous chapter about the relevance and effectiveness of dramatic practices such as exorcising demons or binding Satan. Please don't misunderstand. I do believe that Christians have the authority and ability to thwart Satan's plan to destroy us.

In this final chapter, I want to offer you six practical ways you can exercise God's power without exorcising demons, keeping Satan on the run in your life.

Receive Christ as Your Savior

There is a vast difference between ownership and influence. If I owned a fast-food restaurant, I would control that business. I could decide whom to hire, when to open and close, what prices to charge, and what items to place on the menu.

However, as a small shareholder in McDonald's, my influence over thousands of hamburger outlets is minuscule. Yes, I could attend the annual stockholder meetings and even address the meeting if called upon, but my paltry number of shares makes it unlikely that I would be taken seriously. Only if I acquired a large percentage of the company's stock could I exert any real change in the corporation.

The difference between demon possession and demonic influence is more than theological hairsplitting. While it is true that Satan and his demons can exert varying degrees of influence in a Christian's life, they have no real authority over him because he is God's possession, not Satan's. Their number of *shares* in a Christian's life is limited to whatever percentage of control a believer yields to them. They are influencers, not owners. Paul describes how the Holy Spirit is God's mark of ownership and seal of protection for a Christian:

> In Him, you also, after listening to the message of truth, the gospel of
> your salvation—having also believed, you were sealed in Him with the
> Holy Spirit of promise, who is given as a pledge of our inheritance,
> with a view to the redemption of God's own possession, to the praise
> of His glory. (Ephesians 1:13–14)

The single most effective action you can take to thwart Satan's plan for you and to negate his power over you is to trust in Christ as your Savior. Read carefully these words of the apostle John about the key to overcoming the forces of darkness in this present world:

> For whatever is born of God overcomes the world; and this is the victory that has overcome the world—our faith.
> Who is the one who overcomes the world, but he who believes that Jesus is the Son of God? (1 John 5:4–5)

Can you point to a time when you humbled yourself before God, confessed your need for forgiveness, and said, "God, I believe You sent Your Son,

Jesus, to die on the cross for me. Right now I am trusting in His death to save me from my sins"?

If you are not sure, why not pause right here and pray a similar prayer to your heavenly Father? The moment you receive God's gift of forgiveness, you drive a stake through the heart of Satan's plan for your life. Ownership of your life is immediately transferred from the Prince of Darkness to the Father of Lights. You are no longer a slave of Satan, but you become a child of God.

Refuse to Participate in Any Occult Practices

The word *occult* means "secret" or "hidden" and refers to the practice of seeking a supernatural experience apart from God. Make no mistake about it. You can experience what appear to be miracles apart from God. Such extraordinary events are some of Satan's most effective enticements that lure people into following him. The Bible warns against three specific categories of occult practices that Christians are to avoid.

Divinations are attempts to ascertain the future apart from God's revelation. Various forms of divination include horoscopes, Ouija boards, and astrology. Deuteronomy 18 warns:

> There shall not be found among you anyone who makes his son or his daughter pass through the fire, one who uses divination, one who practices witchcraft.... For whoever does these things is detestable to the LORD. (verses 10, 12)

Magic relies on supernatural power apart from God to produce supernatural results. By magic, I'm not referring to performing card tricks or pulling rabbits out of a hat. In the Bible, magic is the use of Satan's power to produce real, not illusionary, miracles. Exodus 7–11 records that Pharaoh's court magicians were able to duplicate many of Moses's miracles in their attempt to diminish Moses's authority. Since such power obviously did not come from

God (why would He compete against Himself in a "My miracle is better than yours" contest?), only one other source of power is possible.

During the days of the Great Tribulation, the beast and the false prophet will also have supernatural power to perform miracles and deceive the masses, according to Revelation 13:11–15. The false prophet, whose job is to encourage people to worship the beast (whom we refer to as Antichrist), "deceives those who dwell on the earth because of the signs which *it was given him to perform* in the presence of the beast" (Revelation 13:14). Who would grant the false prophet this supernatural power that promotes the worship of Antichrist? You get one guess.

If Satan empowered people to perform miracles in the past and will do so again in the future, why is anyone surprised that he uses the same tactic today to encourage people to serve him rather than God?

One summer more than twenty-five years ago, my college roommate and I went to California for a graduation trip. While there, we went to a taping of a popular television talk show. The usual host was on vacation and the substitute host was the late actor and movie director Orson Welles. Welles, known in his latter years for his interest in the occult, started the show by performing some magical feats. Dressed completely in black, he called for an audience member to come forward. We watched in astonishment as Welles was able to levitate the volunteer several feet off the ground.

A viewer at home might have assumed that there were some optical effects or hidden wires behind the trick. But those of us in the audience could plainly see this was no illusion. During the performance, the studio became unusually cold, and there was an inexplicably eerie feeling in the room. My roommate and I sensed that something was not right, and we quickly got up and left. We had witnessed a true supernatural event but had no interest in being exposed any longer to the power behind it.

Spiritism is the attempt to contact the spirits of the deceased in order to receive comfort or knowledge from the dead. Even today in some high-profile murder cases, you will hear accounts of relatives attempting to contact the victim to discover who committed the crime.

Although Satan has the power to use divination and magic to deceive people, does he possess the ability to facilitate conversations with the dead? Once someone dies and his spirit goes to either Hades (the temporary destination of unbelievers as they await the final judgment) or into the presence of Christ, does Satan have any authority over that person's spirit?

While the answer to that question is debatable, what is clear is that God prohibits any attempt to contact the dead (see Leviticus 20:6). In fact, God may choose to judge those who violate this command by granting them their desire! This is what happened when King Saul attempted to contact the spirit of the prophet Samuel through the witch at En-dor (see 1 Samuel 28 for the complete story). For God's own reason, He allowed Samuel's spirit to communicate with Saul, surprising even the witch! God used Samuel's spirit to voice His own displeasure with Saul for violating the ban on spiritism and for other acts of disobedience, and to announce His judgment on Saul.

As we saw earlier, your mind is the battlefield on which the war for your soul is being waged. If Satan can control your thoughts, he can effectively control your life. Divination, magic, and spiritism are channels through which the Enemy can infiltrate and manipulate your mind. That is why Christians who are serious about defeating the forces of darkness will always avoid these practices.

Renounce Satan and His Demons

By renouncing Satan and his demons, I am not referring to removing them from us through exorcism but removing ourselves from them. We do this by breaking any kind of agreement we may have made in the past with the forces of darkness.

When I began to study this principle, I'll admit I was a little skeptical. Covenants with the devil? Maybe in the movies or in some third-world cultures where superstition runs rampant, but certainly no enlightened person would ever do such a thing. Yet as I reflected more on this idea, I remembered a Saturday afternoon when, as I five-year-old, I lay on the top bunk of my bed during a mother-imposed nap. Not being able to fall asleep, for some reason I decided to enter into a conversation with the devil. I remember the distinct sensation that what I was doing was wrong, but I continued in as much defiance as a five-year-old could muster.

Someone might argue, "That's inconsequential. You were only five and exploring natural childhood curiosities." If that experience were so meaningless, why do I remember it so vividly forty-five years later? A few years ago, recalling that event, I decided that it was important to deal with it once and for all. "Satan, regardless of what I may have said to you, or any agreement I may have made with you," I announced, "I am renouncing you in the name of Jesus Christ, and I am dedicating myself to following Him." I realize that this declaration did not bind or rebuke Satan so that I would be forever free of his influence in my life. The power of this simple act is not in what it did to Satan but what it did for me. I felt released from a mistake made many years ago.

Children are not the only ones who carry on conversations with the devil. Sometimes adults, out of bitter disappointment with God, turn to Satan for help. "Satan, since I can't depend on God, I'm asking you to help me." They rationalize such rebellion by reasoning that God's inattentiveness to their needs leaves them no other choice. I believe that kind of disillusionment was at the root of Saul's rebellion. We saw how King Saul resorted to witchcraft to receive the information he sought. Ironically, the Scriptures record that "Saul had removed from the land those who were mediums and spiritists" (1 Samuel 28:3). The king knew that spiritism was in direct violation of God's commands. So why did he seek to communicate with a dead prophet, knowing he was disobeying God's prohibition?

> When Saul inquired of the LORD, the LORD did not answer him, either by dreams or by Urim or by prophets. (1 Samuel 28:6)

One can almost hear Saul saying to God and/or to himself, "If the Lord will not provide an answer when I want it, I'll find someone who will!" No wonder Samuel observed, "For rebellion is as the sin of divination" (1 Samuel 15:23). The one who seeks information, power, or blessing from Satan often does so in defiance of God, who may have disappointed him.

Can you recall a time in your life when you may have made such an agreement with Satan? If so, you may need to stop here and pray a prayer similar to the one I offered.

Do you know someone who seems enslaved to demonic forces as evidenced by powerful addictions in his life? More effective than attempting to remove demonic spirits from that person would be helping him extricate himself from any kind of covenant he may have entered into with the forces of darkness by making the same kind of declaration I did several years ago.

If you sense that someone is under demonic influence, ask him if he has ever made any kind of agreement with Satan. Usually, most people will answer "no." But if the person can recall some contact he has attempted in the past with the forces of darkness, encourage him to break that agreement. How?

Whether a Christian should directly address Satan as I did a few years ago is debatable. Frankly, since Satan is now a defeated adversary and we have the Holy Spirit residing in us, I see no reason to be afraid of him. But if you don't feel comfortable counseling someone to address Satan directly, it is always appropriate to encourage the person to pray a prayer like this: "God, whatever agreement I may have made with Satan in the past, I am renouncing it now and am dedicating myself completely to obeying You."

RELY ON PRAYER

Some may wonder why I didn't devote an entire chapter to the subject of prayer as some other books on spiritual warfare do. I did this for the same reason a book on dressing for success doesn't begin, "Chapter 1: Remember to Breathe." Even though breathing is essential to any task you undertake, including putting on clothes, it is also assumed.

Prayer is to our spiritual existence what breathing is to our physical existence.

It is one of the four conduits through which God's power flows into our lives (a subject I address fully in my book *I Want More!*). Although Paul did not mention prayer as one of the six pieces of spiritual armor described in Ephesians 6, the apostle viewed prayer as essential to using the armor he had just described:

> With all prayer and petition pray at all times in the Spirit, and with this in view, be on the alert with all perseverance and petition for all the saints. (Ephesians 6:18)

How often should we pray? We should pray as often as we breathe: at all times! "Pray without ceasing," Paul commanded in 1 Thessalonians 5:17. But what exactly is the relationship between prayer and success in spiritual warfare?

First, let's debunk a popular myth about prayer and spiritual warfare. God's power is not limited by our prayers. God and His angels do not require a certain level of "prayer cover" before they can work. God's plan, which includes His ultimate victory over Satan, cannot be thwarted by anyone or anything, including our lack of prayer:

> Our God is in the heavens;
> He does whatever He pleases. (Psalm 115:3)

> I know that you can do anything,
> and no one can stop you. (Job 42:2, NLT)

Then why is prayer essential to success in our struggle against Satan? Why should we bother to pray if God is going to do whatever He pleases anyway? There is a simple answer: because the Word of God commands us to. The apostle Paul was a strong believer in the sovereignty of God:

> So then it does not depend on the man who wills or the man who runs, but on God who has mercy. (Romans 9:16)

But the same Paul, who believed everything depends upon God, also believed that the prayers of the Roman Christians could change the course of his ministry:

> Now I urge you, brethren, by our Lord Jesus Christ and by the love
> of the Spirit, to strive together with me in your prayers to God for
> me, that I may be rescued from those who are disobedient in Judea.
> (Romans 15:30–31)

The relationship between prayer, God's sovereign will, and spiritual warfare is a mystery impossible to unravel this side of heaven. Nevertheless, one can see how three particular ingredients of prayer can be effective in diffusing the spiritual hand grenades Satan lobs our way.

One component of effective prayer is *thanksgiving* (see Philippians 4:6). Expressing gratitude for what God has already done for us extinguishes one of Satan's favorite flaming arrows, the arrow of discontent. The Enemy loves to focus our attention on what we don't have, on that one piece of fruit that is still beyond our reach until getting it becomes an obsession. Taking time to recount all that God has done for us helps restore a balanced perspective to our lives, making us less susceptible to the Enemy's bait.

Confession is another essential part of prayer. In the model prayer, Jesus instructed us to ask God to "forgive us our debts" (Matthew 6:12). How does confession of sins protect us from Satan's advances into our lives? This is so simple it is almost embarrassing to write. It's practically impossible to be confessing sin and practicing sin at the same time. As John Ortberg points out, when we sin, we're asking God to turn His back so we can continue the disobedient behavior we started.[1]

I want to watch this movie by myself in my hotel room.
I'm going to give my mate a piece of my mind.
I will pad my expense account when I have a chance.

On the other hand, by acknowledging our failures to God, we are saying, "Lord, please don't hide Yourself from me any longer. I need You desperately.

Here's where I've been wrong. Forgive me, and help me not to make the same mistake again." This kind of confession is the first step in putting on the breast-plate of practiced righteousness.

A third component of prayer is *petition,* in which we ask God to do something for us or for someone else. Paul regularly prayed for spiritual discernment for others, for protection from evildoers and the spiritual powers behind them, and for boldness in sharing the gospel of Christ.

> Finally, brethren, pray for us that the word of the Lord will spread
> rapidly and be glorified, just as it did also with you; and that we will be
> rescued from perverse and evil men; for not all have faith. (2 Thessalo-
> nians 3:1–2)

Again, I do not understand the relationship between prayer and God's sovereignty, but the fact that even Jesus prayed to our Father to "deliver us from evil" (Matthew 6:13) suggests that prayer can shield us from Satan's attacks. I would encourage you to regularly ask God for protection in spiritual warfare with prayers similar to the following.

A Prayer for Yourself

Dear Heavenly Father:

I realize that without Your power and protection I am no match for the attacks of the Evil One. I pray today for discernment to recognize the multiple ways he is going to attempt to enter my life. I confess that I have failed You by _____, but today I ask for Your forgiveness, and I resolve to obey You in every area of my life. I claim the power of Your Holy Spirit, Who has freed me from the power of sin. Help me throughout the day to remember that I have no obligation to obey Satan or to give in to my old desires. I pray that through my obedience Your name would be glorified throughout my life.

In Jesus's name, I pray.

A Prayer for Your Family

Dear Heavenly Father:

You have been so good to bless me with a wonderful mate and children. They are gifts from You. I ask You to protect _____ from any accident or illness that would destroy his/her life. I pray You would use Your angels to bring assistance to _____ as needed throughout the day. Above all, I pray today for _____. Open his/her eyes to the real forces of Satan that are working to discourage and defeat. Help _____ to remember that he/she is no longer a slave to sin. Give him both the desire and the power to obey You in every decision made today. I pray that _____ will walk in a manner worthy of You, bearing fruit in every good work.

In Jesus's name, I pray.

A Prayer for Someone Under Satan's Influence

Dear Heavenly Father:

I come before You on behalf of _____. As much as I love _____, I realize that You love him/her even more. I believe that although _____ belongs to You, he/she has been deceived by the Enemy. I pray that You would open _____ spiritual eyes so that he/she might see clearly how Satan has deceived and enslaved. Remind _____ of the power You have granted him to break free of the Enemy's grip. Help me as I talk with him/her to find that balance between compassion and frankness.

In Jesus's name, I pray.

RESIST SATAN'S ATTEMPTS TO INFLUENCE YOUR LIFE

I have some good news and some bad news for you. The bad news is that you have a powerful adversary who possesses an ironclad resolve to destroy you. The good news? God has already provided you with the resources you need to resist your adversary. While there is no evidence in the Bible that we have the power to bind Satan or exorcise his demons, we are commanded to resist the devil.

> Submit therefore to God. *Resist* the devil and he will flee from you. (James 4:7)

> Be of sober spirit, be on the alert. Your adversary, the devil, prowls around like a roaring lion, seeking someone to devour. But *resist* him, firm in your faith. (1 Peter 5:8–9)

"Robert, that sounds so simple," you say, "but how do I resist Satan?"

Let's take a moment and review each of the pieces of spiritual equipment God has provided you to deflect the attacks of the Enemy. Allow me to offer a practical step of action for each one.

- **Belt of Truth.** To which of Satan's four favorite mind games described in chapter 7, "Satan's Favorite Mind Games," do you tend to be most susceptible? Memorize the suggested scripture passage to use in confronting these deceptions.

- **Breastplate of Righteousness**. Complete the obedience inventory in chapter 9. You now have an intensely specific action plan to follow that will provide you with the benefits and protection that come from obedience.

- **Spiritual Footwear.** Identify one person in your circle of influence (family, friends, work associates) whom you would like to see become a Christian in the next six months. Begin to pray each day for his salvation, invite him to special events at your church, look for opportunities to pepper your conversation with spiritual salt that would increase his interest in knowing Jesus, and take advantage of any opportunity to share how to become a Christian.

- **Shield of Faith.** Having faith is believing God will do what He has promised and then acting accordingly. In what one area of your life are you finding it difficult to obey God, even though you know exactly what you should do? Resolve that you are going to move forward in faith regardless of the consequences, believing that God will eventually reward you.

- **Helmet of Salvation.** Becoming a Christian not only saves you from the *penalty* of sin but also delivers you from the *power* of sin. Satan no longer has ownership of your life. You are no longer under any obligation to serve him or to give in to your old nature. To remind yourself of this truth, memorize Romans 6:11–12: "Even so consider yourselves to be dead to sin, but alive to God in Christ Jesus. Therefore do not let sin reign in your mortal body so that you obey its lusts."

- **Sword of the Spirit.** God's Word has the power to free you from flawed thinking that leads to wrong behavior. Do you have a plan for a regular intake of God's Word? Consider purchasing a *One Year Bible* that will allow you to read from both the Old and New Testaments each day. If you are a slower reader, these programs can be extended to two years so that you are not rushing though the Bible to meet an artificial deadline. If those types of programs do not appeal to you, then select a book of the New Testament that you will read through each day of the month for thirty days. Most books of the New Testament can be read completely in twenty minutes or less. Trust me, once you have read a book thirty times, you will find yourself thinking about certain passages without having to memorize them. You might start with Ephesians, the letters of Peter, and Philippians. For longer books like Romans, you can divide them in halves or even thirds.

Remember these are not just my ideas for how you might succeed in your spiritual battle against Satan. God promises that any Christian who puts on these pieces of spiritual armor *will* defeat Satan's blueprint for the believer's destruction.

REMEMBER THAT VICTORY IS POSSIBLE

At some point in the writing of any book, the author is asked to provide the marketing department with a one-sentence summary of the book. My summary is this: every Christian is in a life-and-death struggle with a formidable but defeatable opponent. Above all else, remember:

- **The war is intense.** Any pause in Satan's attacks is simply an attempt to lull you into a false sense of security while he reloads.
- **The Enemy is determined.** He has a carefully crafted plan for your defeat. The spiritual battlefield is strewn with the corpses of Christians who have underestimated his resolve and his resources.
- **The stakes are high.** Your success or defeat will reverberate throughout eternity.
- **You can win.** God has already provided you with every resource you need to prevail against the Enemy.

The spiritual battle in which you are engaged is real. In fact, this invisible war is the reality behind many of the conflicts you confront every day of your life. But there is no need to panic. God has provided you with every piece of armor you need to overcome your already-defeated adversary.

It's time to wake up.

Put on.

Stand firm.

And move forward with your divine defense.

QUESTIONS

For personal study or small-group discussion

Chapter 1: The Other World

1. What experiences in your life led you to believe in the existence of another, invisible world?

2. Why do you think some people have difficulty accepting the reality of the spirit world?

3. Do you accept or reject the author's belief that most Christians are unaware of a spirit world alive and active all around us? What are the consequences of failing to understand the reality of this invisible world?

4. What are the two reasons the author gives for the necessity of understanding the reality of the other world?

5. Think for a few moments about the conflicts you have experienced in the past week. Do you think any of these conflicts are ultimately attributable to Satan? Why or why not?

6. Why do you think some Christians are reluctant to study the subject of spiritual warfare?

7. If people really believed they were in a life-and-death struggle against Satan and his forces, what differences would it make in how they lived?

8. Why did you decide to read this book? What do you hope to gain from this study of spiritual warfare?

Chapter 2: The Purpose-Driven Strife

1. Do you accept the author's contention that our lives are small parts in a cosmic drama being played out for an invisible audience? Why or why not?

2. Outside of the Bible, what evidence is there for the existence of Satan?

3. What have you learned about Satan that you did not realize until you read this chapter?

4. Explain how you would answer this question: "Why did God create Satan if He knew that Satan would cause so much trouble?"

5. The author claims, "Whenever you ask yourself what you really want in life, you're in danger of making the same mistake that led to Satan's removal from heaven." Do you agree or disagree? Why?

6. Do you think Satan knows he will ultimately be defeated? If not, why not? If so, why do you think he continues his assault on God's kingdom?

7. Which phrase better describes planet Earth: this is my Father's world or this is enemy-occupied territory? Why?

8. Have you tended to give too much or too little attention to the reality of Satan in your life? What new insight have you gained from reading this chapter?

Chapter 3: Blueprint for Your Destruction

1. Imagine you are Satan. Describe the plan you would design to ensure the downfall of a Christian who bears your name. *hit me when I'm tired / stressed* *guilt*

2. Describe a time in your life when you were especially discouraged. Did discouragement draw you closer to God or alienate you from God? How did that reaction help you deal with discouragement?

3. Which of the three entangling weeds mentioned by Jesus in Luke 8:14 is the major distraction in your life: worries, riches, or pleasure? Has this always been true or has your primary distraction changed through the years? How?

4. Why is the love of money "Spiritual Enemy #1" to your relationship with God? Are the wealthy more susceptible to this distraction than the poor? Why or why not? *They can afford more*

5. Are you more inclined to overindulge yourself with pleasure or rob yourself of pleasure? Whatever your answer, how does Satan use this extreme to his advantage in your life?

6. What unsatisfied desires in your life, such as recognition, sexual fulfillment, or financial security, could Satan easily take advantage of? *loneliness* Describe how you think God would like those needs to be satisfied.

7. The author mentions four specific times when you're most vulnerable to Satan's temptations: when you've experienced success, when you're tired, when you're alone, and when you're waiting on God. During which of those four times do you find yourself most likely to give in to temptation? What are some practical ways you can guard yourself during those times?

8. If you are married, think about your mate for a moment. When and in what areas is he or she most vulnerable to Satan's attacks? What needs are prevalent in your spouse's life that you can fulfill?

Chapter 4: Demons in the World Today

1. Do you think Christians give too little or too much attention to the subject of demons? Why is that?

2. Why do you think there are so few references to demons in the Old Testament?

3. Are demons as active in the world today as they were in New Testament times? Why or why not?

4. What reason does the author give for the high degree of demonic activity recorded in the gospels? Do you agree? Are there other reasons you would suggest?

5. Why do you think the Bible does not clearly explain the origin of demons? Do you agree with the author's conclusion that they are fallen angels? Why or why not?

6. The author makes the bold assertion that demonic forces use religions such as Islam, Mormonism, and Buddhism to prevent unbelievers from coming to Christ. Do you agree or disagree with his statement? Why?

7. Do you think an unbeliever's rejection of the gospel is mainly attributable to his own choice, demonic activity, or some other factor? Explain why.

8. What did you learn about demons from this chapter that you didn't already know? Are you more or less concerned about them now? Why?

Chapter 5: What Demons Want to Do to You

1. How do you reconcile God's sovereignty over all His creation with the fact that Satan is "the prince of the power of the air" (Ephesians 2:2)?

2. Have you ever experienced an illness that you attributed to satanic attack? Do you think it is possible to determine the cause of a physical illness? Why or why not?

3. How would you respond to someone who argued that people described in the gospels as being demonically influenced were suffering from mental disorders? Is it possible to distinguish between mental disorders and demonic influence? If so, how?

4. Suppose a friend came to you suffering from severe depression and suicidal thoughts and asked, "Do you think I am under demonic attack?" How would you respond? What advice would you offer?

5. Do you believe that suicide is an unforgivable sin? Why or why not? What would you say to comfort someone whose loved one had committed suicide?

6. How can a Christian possess the Holy Spirit but also be used by Satan?

7. Do you know of a time when Satan or his demons used you as an instrument in someone else's life? What would you do differently to change that?

8. What is the difference between being *demon possessed* and *demon influenced*?

Chapter 6: Winning the Mind Games

1. Why do you think Christians are not more intentional in preparing for spiritual warfare?
2. The author mentions four channels Satan uses to influence our thoughts. Which one do you think is Satan's most effective channel of communication? Why?
3. Do you agree that Satan can use Christians to influence our thoughts? Why or why not?
4. If you agree, can you cite an instance in your life when Satan used a Christian to communicate a message to you?

Chapter 7: Satan's Favorite Mind Games

1. What makes discontent such an effective tool for Satan? Has he ever used the "You don't have what you need to be happy" lie on you? How did you deal with it?
2. Read 1 Timothy 6:6–8. What does Paul imply is a major cause of discontent? Describe the relationship between expectations and contentment.
3. Why is it so easy to believe that we control our destiny? What situations in life remind us that we do not control our destiny?
4. Do you believe the Christian culture has adopted and legitimized Satan's lie "You are in control of your own destiny"? How so?
5. Explain the relationship between independence from God and fear in a person's life.
6. Can fear be helpful in someone's relationship with God? Why or why not?
7. How does Satan use the attitude of bitterness to enslave us and rob us?
8. Is it possible to forgive someone who has not asked you for forgiveness? Why or why not? How does Jesus answer that question in Mark 11:25–26?

Chapter 8: When Satan Comes Knocking

1. Do you agree with the author's statement that we are not always responsible for the wrong thoughts that enter our minds? Why or why not?

2. How can we control harmful thoughts that attempt to seize control of our minds?

3. What insights did you gain from the account of Jesus's temptation in the wilderness? Explain the difference between temptation and sin.

4. How is a toehold different from a stronghold? Are there any thoughts in your life that have moved from being toeholds to footholds or strongholds?

5. Imagine you are the teacher of a sixth-grade Sunday-school class. How would you explain to twelve-year-olds the importance of recognizing wrong thoughts and replacing them with spiritual thoughts?

6. Which of the following wrong thoughts most often attempts entry into your mind: discontent, immorality, or fear? Find a verse in the Bible (other than the ones the author cited) to replace each of these wrong thoughts:

   Fear:

   Discontent:

   Immorality:

7. Why do you think so many Christians believe it is impossible to win Satan's mind games?

8. What is the most helpful insight you gained from this chapter? What do you intend to do differently as a result of that insight?

Chapter 9: Putting Out the NOT WELCOME Mat

1. Explain why the "belt of truth" is the first piece of spiritual armor Paul describes in Ephesians 6.

2. Before you read this chapter, did you have an idea of what Paul meant by the piece of armor called the "breastplate of righteousness"? If so, has your understanding changed as a result of this chapter? How?

3. What is the difference between self-righteousness, imputed righteousness, and practiced righteousness? Do you think Christians tend to give too much or too little emphasis to practiced righteousness? Why?

4. Do you believe Christians should have to work at obedience or should obedience come naturally?

5. How did this chapter change your understanding of Romans 6:23: "The wages of sin is death"?

6. If someone said, "I believe God will treat all Christians the same in heaven," how would you respond? Is earning rewards in heaven a proper motivation for obedience? Why or why not?

7. If you were standing before the judgment seat of Christ, what would the Lord commend you for? What would you wish you had done differently?

8. The author states that most of us prefer the miraculous to the mundane. Do you agree or disagree with the author's belief that, in dealing with our problems, we Christians are more attracted to supernatural deliverance than self-discipline? Why?

Chapter 10: Putting on Your Soul Soles

1. The author writes, "The spiritual boots that give stability to a Christian's life are his willingness and ability to share the message of Christ with others." Do you agree? Why or why not?

2. Why do you think so few Christians share their faith with others? When was the last time you explained to someone how to become a Christian?

3. If someone were to ask you, "Since God is going to save whomever He chooses to save, why do I need to share my faith with anyone?" how would you answer?

4. How does adopting God's purpose as your life purpose protect you against Satan's scheme to destroy you?

5. According to the author, a clear purpose can motivate you to make three critical choices that will protect you against the Enemy's attack: purity, generosity, diligence. Which of the three choices do you think is most important? Why?

6. Do you believe that faith in Jesus Christ is the only way a person can be saved? Why or why not? What effect does your belief have on your motivation to share your faith?

7. If someone said to you, "I think Dr. Jeffress should have added a fifth point in his presentation of the gospel: *we need to obey Christ in every area of our life*," would you agree? Why or why not?

8. Take a moment and think about your friends, co-workers, and family members. Does anyone who may not be a Christian come to mind? Begin to pray for him right now. Ask God to make you sensitive to opportunities to share the message of Christ.

Chapter 11: Storming the Gates of Hell

1. Reread Matthew 16:18: "Upon this rock I will build My church; and the gates of Hades will not overpower it." What are the practical implications of acting proactively rather than reactively in relation to Satan and his kingdom?

2. Do you believe Christians should openly rebuke Satan or attempt to bind the devil? Why or why not?

3. Did the author's imagery of walking along a street lined with demons trying to discourage, distract, or confuse you have an impact on you? How so? How have Satan and his demons been most successful in stopping you—or at least slowing you down—in your Christian walk?

4. How does the author's definition of faith differ from the common understanding of faith? Do you agree with his definition? If so, how should that understanding affect your prayer life?

5. What is the relationship between assurance of salvation and success in spiritual warfare?

6. Which is harder for you to believe: that you have been saved from the penalty of sin or that you have been saved from the power of sin? Why?

7. What is the most important insight you gained from this chapter about what Paul calls the "sword of the spirit"? Identify specific actions you could take to become more skilled in your use of this sword.

8. Reflect on the six pieces of spiritual armor discussed in Ephesians 6. Which piece of armor has been your greatest defense against Satan's plan to destroy you? Which piece(s) of armor do you most often neglect to put on or use?

Chapter 12: Exercise Power or Exorcise Demons?

1. Have you ever experienced a personal encounter with a demonic force? What made you think you were dealing with demonic activity?

2. Do you believe the ability to exorcise demons was limited to Jesus, the twelve apostles, and a few others in the New Testament? Why or why not?

3. Contrast the way Jesus exorcised demons with the way exorcisms are portrayed today. How do you explain the difference?

4. Do you agree with the author's statement, "While it is true that all of the Bible was written *for* us, not all of it was written to us" (page 170). How can you determine which promises or commands in the Bible directly apply to you?

5. Why do you believe there is a resurgence of interest in demonic activity among Christians and non-Christians? Do you think this is good? Why or why not?

6. Assuming you had the ability to exorcise demons from individuals, in what ways is the exorcism limited according to Luke 11:24–26?

7. Is it wrong to question the legitimacy of those claiming to perform exorcisms today? Why or why not? If you believe that God has not commanded and empowered Christians to perform exorcisms, how do you explain what is occurring?

8. The author states that the single most important factor in demonic control is a person's choices. Do you agree or disagree? Why?

Chapter 13: Using the Divine Defense

1. How is Satan's ability to control an individual altered when that person becomes a Christian?

2. What would you say to someone who says, "Because I am a Christian I don't need to worry about Satan's attacks against me"?

3. Why does the Bible warn against participation in occult practices? Have you seen other people affected by their participation in the occult? If so, what were the consequences?

4. Is Satan's power to perform miracles limited? Why or why not? Why do you think God has granted Satan the ability to perform miracles?

5. How does the author differentiate between exorcising demons and renouncing Satan?

6. As you review each of the six pieces of spiritual armor, which one do you tend to use most often? Why? Which piece of armor do you need to become more proficient in using?

7. Who in your circle of friends or family members do you sense is under spiritual attack? Will you commit to praying for that person each day this next month? Beyond prayer, what insight from this book would be helpful to share?

8. In one or two sentences, summarize the most important insight you have gained from this book. Identify the one or two things you could do differently in your life that would give you the greatest success in the divine defense.

NOTES

Chapter 1

1. Cited in Philip Yancey, *Rumors of Another World: What on Earth Are We Missing?* (Grand Rapids, MI: Zondervan, 2003), 186.
2. Randy Alcorn, *In Light of Eternity: Perspectives on Heaven* (Colorado Springs: WaterBrook, 1999), 25.
3. Cited in Yancey, *Rumors of Another World,* 161.
4. Gregory A. Boyd, *God at War: The Bible and Spiritual Conflict* (Downers Grove, IL: InterVarsity, 1997), 19, 55.
5. Charles R. Swindoll, *Hope Again: When Life Hurts and Dreams Fade* (Dallas: Word, 1996), 168.
6. D. Martyn Lloyd-Jones, *The Christian Warfare* (Grand Rapids, MI: Baker, 1977), 41–2.
7. Stu Weber, *Spirit Warriors*: *A Soldier Looks at Spiritual Warfare* (Sisters, OR: Multnomah, 2001), 16.
8. Steven J. Lawson, *Faith Under Fire: Standing Strong When Satan Attacks* (Wheaton, IL: Crossway, 1995), xi.
9. Lyrics from "I'm in Lord's Army," traditional. Copyright unknown.
10. John Eldredge, *Wild at Heart: Discovering the Passionate Soul of a Man* (Nashville: Thomas Nelson, 2001), 49.
11. R. Kent Hughes, *Luke,* (Wheaton, IL: Crossway, 1998), 1:303.
12. Cited in Hughes, *Luke,* 303–4.
13. Neil Anderson, *The Bondage Breaker* (Eugene, OR: Harvest, 2000), 93.
14. Cited in Weber, *Spirit Warriors,* 14.

Chapter 2

1. Kenneth L. Woodward with David Gates, "Giving the Devil His Due," *Newsweek,* August 30, 1982, 74.

2. J. Dwight Pentecost, *Your Adversary the Devil* (Grand Rapids: Zondervan, 1969), introduction.

3. Preachingtoday.com, "President's Surprise Thanksgiving Visit Recalls Incarnation," www.preachingtoday.com, November 27, 2003.

Chapter 3

1. Andrea Gerlin, Peter Smolowitz, Steven Thomma, "Armor's Arrival Catches City's Defenders Off Guard," *Miami Herald*, April 6, 2003.

2. Rajiv Chandrasekaran and Peter Baker, "Troops, Tanks Attack Central Baghdad," *Washington Post*, April 7, 2003.

3. Stu Weber, *Spirit Warriors: A Soldier Looks at Spiritual Warfare* (Sisters, OR: Multnomah, 2001), 143–44.

4. Donald Grey Barnhouse, *The Invisible War* (Grand Rapids: Zondervan, 1965), 51.

5. Cited in A. L. Williams, *All You Can Do Is All You Can Do but All You Can Do Is Enough* (New York: Ivy Books, 1988), 224.

6. Cited in Charles R. Swindoll, *Job: A Man of Heroic Endurance* (Nashville: W Publishing, 2004), 42.

7. Cited in Robert Jeffress, *When Forgiveness Doesn't Make Sense* (Colorado Springs: WaterBrook, 2000), 195.

8. C. S. Lewis, *The Screwtape Letters* (New York: Macmillan, 1961), 64–65.

9. Alexis de Tocqueville, *Democracy in America* (electronic edition, June 1, 1997, from Henry Reeve translation, 1899), www.tocqueville.org.

10. Lewis, *The Screwtape Letters*, 49.

11. John Eldredge, *Wild at Heart: Discovering the Passionate Soul of a Man* (Nashville: Thomas Nelson, 2001), 170.

12. Oscar Wilde, *The Picture of Dorian Gray* (e-book: www.online-literature.com), chapter 2.

Chapter 6

1. Jere Longman, *Among the Heroes: Flight 93 and the Passengers and Crew Who Fought Back* (New York: HarperCollins, 2002), 38–39.

2. Cited in John Ortberg, *The Life You've Always Wanted* (Grand Rapids, MI: Zondervan, 2002), 175.

3. Cited in Neil Anderson, *The Bondage Breaker* (Eugene, OR: Harvest, 2000), 177–78.

Chapter 7

1. John Ortberg, *God Is Closer than You Think* (Grand Rapids, MI: Zondervan, 2005), 90.

2. Cited in Steve Hubbard, *Faith in Sports: Athletes and Their Religion On and Off the Field* (New York: Doubleday, 1998), 214.

3. William Ernest Henley, "Invictus," in *The Best Loved Poems of the American People,* comp. Hazel Felleman (Garden City, NY: Garden City Books, 1936), 73.

4. Michael Crichton, "Let's Stop Scaring Ourselves," *Parade,* December 5, 2004, 6–7.

Chapter 8

1. Charles F. Stanley, *When the Enemy Strikes: The Keys to Winning Our Spiritual Battles* (Nashville: Thomas Nelson, 2004), 76–77.

2. Neil Anderson, *The Bondage Breaker* (Eugene, OR: Harvest, 2000), 23–24.

3. Anderson, *The Bondage Breaker,* 24.

Chapter 9

1. Cited in Philip Yancey, *Rumors of Another World* (Grand Rapids, MI: Zondervan, 2003), 111.

2. Cited in Erwin Lutzer, *Your Eternal Rewards: Triumph and Tears at the Judgment Seat of Christ* (Chicago: Moody, 1998), 18.

3. Joseph Dillow, *The Reign of the Servant Kings* (Haysville, NC: Schoettle, 1992), 532.

4. C. S. Lewis, *The Screwtape Letters* (New York: Macmillan, 1961), 65.

5. John Maxwell, *Thinking for a Change* (New York: Warner, 2003), 12–13.

6. Dallas Willard, *The Spirit of the Disciplines: Understanding How God Changes Lives* (San Francisco: Harper & Row, 1988), 3–4.

7. Randy Alcorn, *Lord Foulgrin's Letters* (Sisters, OR: Multnomah, 2000), 173–74.

8. Cited in J. Oswald Sanders, *Spiritual Manpower* (Chicago: Moody, 1965), 145.

9. Dallas Willard, *The Divine Conspiracy: Rediscovering Our Hidden Life in God* (San Francisco: HarperSanFrancisco, 1998), 345.

Chapter 10

1. James Carville and Paul Begala, *Buck Up, Suck Up—and Come Back When You Foul Up: 12 Secrets from the War Room* (New York: Simon & Schuster, 2002), 88.

2. *Our Daily Bread,* August 10, 1999.

3. Cited in Joshua Harris, *Stop Dating the Church* (Sisters, OR: Multnomah, 2004), 20.

4. Ravi Zacharias, *Jesus Among Other Gods: The Absolute Claims of the Christian Message* (Nashville: W Publishing, 2000), 13.

5. John Eldredge, *Wild at Heart: Discovering the Passionate Soul of a Man* (Nashville: Thomas Nelson, 2001), 142.

6. Eldredge, *Wild at Heart,* 172.

7. Monique Stuart, "Fire and Brimstone," *Washington Times,* August 3, 2004.

8. Jeffrey L. Sheler, "Faith in America." *U.S. News & World Report,* May 6, 2005, 40–44.

9. Michael Simpson, *Permission Evangelism* (Colorado Springs, CO: NexGen, 2003), 89.

10. Cited in Simpson, *Permission Evangelism,* 149.

Chapter 11

1. Adapted from Neil Anderson, *The Bondage Breaker* (Eugene, OR: Harvest, 2000), 118–19.

Chapter 12

1. Charles Ryrie, *Ryrie Study Bible* (Chicago: Moody Bible Institute, 1978), 1433.
2. David Neff, "Scott Peck vs. Satan," *Christianity Today*, February 2005, 84.
3. Neff, "Scott Peck vs. Satan," 85.
4. Neil Anderson, *The Bondage Breaker* (Eugene, OR: Harvest, 2000), 256.

Chapter 13

1. John Ortberg, *God Is Closer than You Think* (Grand Rapids, MI: Zondervan, 2005), 41.

ABOUT THE AUTHOR

ROBERT JEFFRESS is a best-selling author of fifteen books, including *The Solomon Secrets, Spirit Wars, Grace Gone Wild!* and *Hell? Yes!* He has served as senior pastor of the 9,500-member First Baptist Church of Wichita Falls, Texas, since 1992; is a graduate of Baylor University, Dallas Theological Seminary, and earned his doctorate at Southwestern Baptist Theological Seminary. Dr. Jeffress hosts the weekly television program *Pathway to Victory,* aired on more than 1,000 television stations and cable systems, and in 13 countries around the world. He and his family live in Wichita Falls, Texas.

ABOUT THE AUTHOR'S MINISTRIES

First Baptist Church of Wichita Falls, Texas, is a Christian evangelical church whose mission is to spread the good news of Jesus Christ and to lead people to become obedient and reproducing disciples of Jesus Christ, as He commanded in Matthew 28:18–20.

The church conducts many ministries from small-group Bible studies (LIFE Groups—Learning, Involving, Fellowshipping, and Evangelizing) and prayer and recovery groups, to community outreach, and women's and teen ministries. Learn more about the church online at the First Baptist Church Web site: www.fbcwf.org.

To tune into the preaching and teaching ministry of Dr. Robert Jeffress, check out *Pathway to Victory,* a nationally broadcast television and radio program. The program can currently be seen on Faith TV, Saturday nights at 6:00 p.m. (CST); and on Family Net TV on Sundays at noon (CST) and the Daystar Network on Sunday afternoons at 1:30 p.m. (CST). The program is heard on radio Monday–Friday in numerous cities. For a complete list of stations and times, visit www.robertjeffress.com. To order tapes from the *Pathway* archive, call toll-free 1-800-348-TAPE.

Designed to provide insight on the truth found in God's word, *Pathway to Victory* aims to give viewers and listeners practical application of God's word for everyday life through clear biblical teaching.

SECOND ACT, SECOND CHANCE

Robert Jeffress invites you to take a sneak peek at his next book, *Second Act, Second Chance: Turning Your Biggest Mess into an Incredible Success.*

Waiting anxiously for my flight to be called so that I could return home, I decided to make one final stop in the rest room. I was washing my hands when I glanced over and saw a woman entering the bathroom. She froze in her tracks upon seeing me at the sink and began to apologize profusely.

"I'm so sorry," she said.

"That's all right," I replied, trying to alleviate her obvious embarrassment. "It happens to me all the time."

I finished drying my hands, brushed my hair, and straightened my tie before leaving. For some reason, I glanced back and noticed an unexpected image on the side of the rest room I just exited: a feminine stick figure. WOMEN, the sign said.

Mistakes! We all make them—just about every hour of every day. I'm sure you have a number of embarrassing moments you could share as well.

However, I imagine the reason you picked up this book is not because of some minor mishap like entering the wrong rest room. In your distant or immediate past is one giant whopper of a mistake that haunts you...

- An innocent friendship that turned into a torrid affair.
- A poor financial decision that threatens your future security.
- An opportunity you squandered because of sheer laziness.
- A choice to invest more time in your career than in your family.
- A decision to end a relationship you should have stayed in.
- A decision to stay in a relationship you should have ended.

Your mistake, along with its accompanying and unending regrets, raises all kinds of questions: can my mistake ever be forgiven? Even if I am forgiven of my mistake, will I still spend the rest of my life paying for that mistake? If God has planned every detail of my life before I was born, did His plan include the mistake I made? Can I totally recover from my mistake?

Well, as the old joke begins, I have some good news and some bad news for you. The bad news is that you can't change history; life has no rewind button. The good news is that your mistake can actually be a steppingstone to greater success in life—and that's what this book is all about.

American novelist F. Scott Fitzgerald once wrote, "There are no second acts in American lives." But he was wrong. You can recover from your mistakes and enjoy a great second act in your life. Your biggest mess can morph into your greatest success by applying the principles from God's Word we are going to discover in this book.

Coming Spring 2007
ISBN 978-1-40000-7091-6

Challenging and provocative resources from Robert Jeffress.

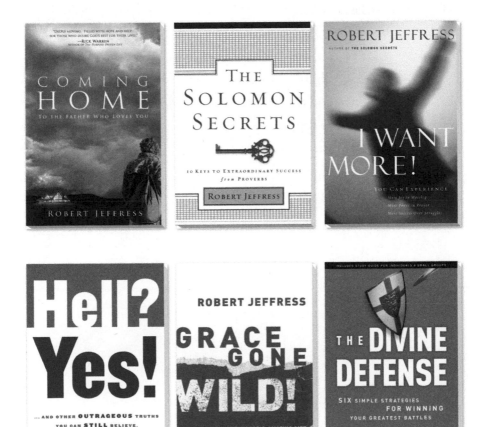